THE

*Two brothers, two motorcycles,
one incredible adventure*

Colin Pyle and Ryan Pyle

Published by G219 Productions Limited
www.G219Productions.com
www.TheIndiaRide.com

The India Ride. Copyright 2013 by G219 Productions Limited
All rights reserved.
ISBN-13: 978-0957576247
ISBN-10: 0957576247

Printed in the United States of America. No part of this book may be used or reproduced in any manner whatsoever without written permission except in the case of brief quotations embodied in critical articles and reviews. For information, address G219 Productions Limited: Suite 4, 62 Chesterton Road, London, W106ER, United Kingdom.

G219 Production books may be purchased for educational, business, or sales promotional use. For information, please write: Special Markets, G219 Productions Limited: Suite 4, 62 Chesterton Road, London, W106ER, United Kingdom.

FIRST EDITION
Designed by Jonathan Hogan
Cover Photograph by Chad Ingraham

Library of Congress Cataloging-in-Publication Data
Pyle, Ryan and Pyle, Colin
The India Ride: Two brothers, two motorcycles, one incredible adventure / Ryan Pyle and Colin Pyle.
p. cm.
ISBN 978-0957576247
1. India – Description and Travel. Adventure. 2. Transportation. India. I. Title

---

Printed in the United States of America

This book is dedicated to the people of India. Thank you for providing us with an experience that taught us much about the spirit, beauty, diversity and complexities that exist within your incredible country.

Contents

1	Why India?	1
2	Setting it up	17
3	Day one	35
4	Paragliding at Manali	45
5	The Saach Pass	55
6	Amritsar to Rajasthan	67
7	The Rat Temple	81
8	They make wine in India	91
9	Pune	101
10	The wonderful Mr Azad	111
11	From Kerala to Puducherry	119
12	Death and frustration on the east coast highway	137
13	Darjeeling	157
14	Ancient India	167
15	The return to modern India	181
16	Lessons and legacies	189
Acknowledgements		207

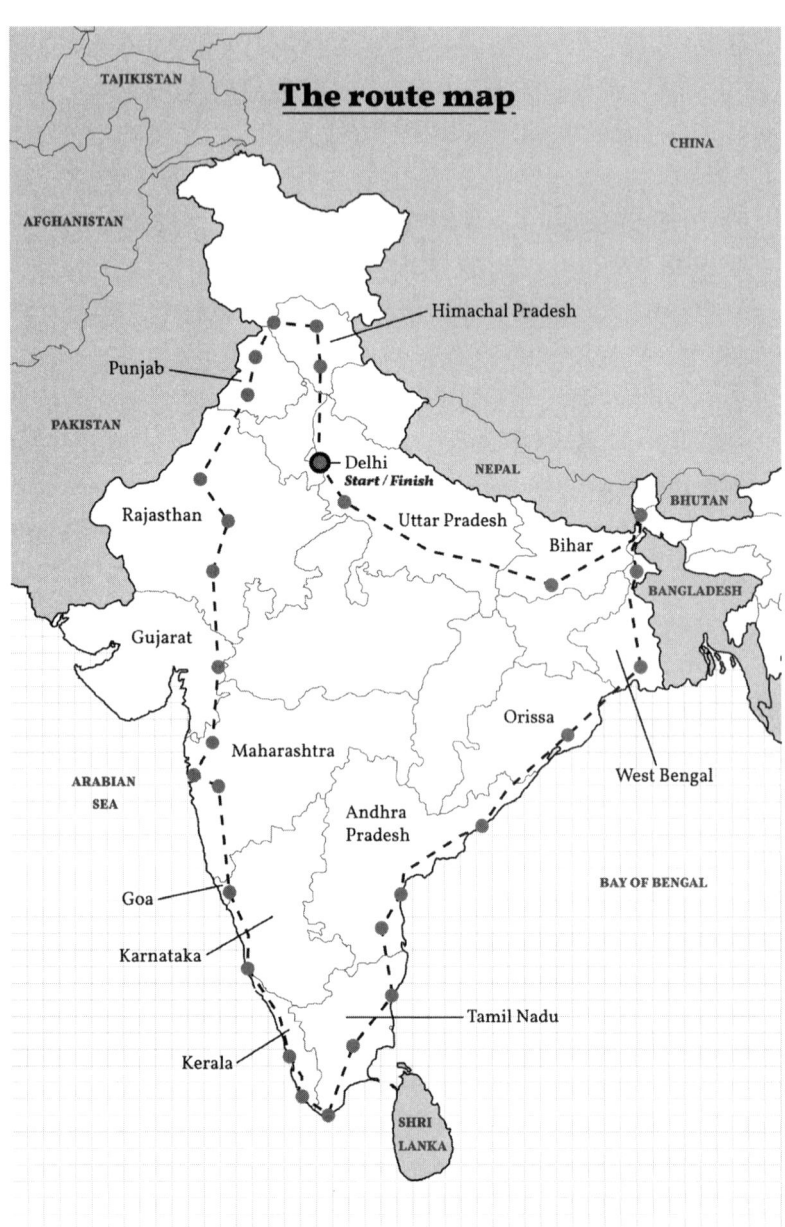

Chapter 1
Why India?

Ryan

In March 2010, when my brother Colin and I met in Central Park, New York, to eat sandwiches together in the sunshine, we ended up making a decision that changed our lives. I was 31 years old, living with my wife and children in Shanghai, China, and working as a freelance photographer, primarily for newspapers and magazines in the US and UK. Colin was 28 and living with his wife in Toronto, Canada, where we'd both grown up and where he was a currency trader in the very successful business he'd created and then sold. He'd known that the transition from calling the shots to working for the boss of what had been *his* company was going to be challenging. What he was finding really difficult to deal with, however, was all the time wasting and inefficiency, which included having to attend several meetings a day, during which all senior-management decisions had to be explained and justified. The pace of business had slowed to a grinding halt.

By the end of that unseasonably warm early-spring afternoon in New York, Colin had decided that, when he returned to Toronto a couple of days later, he was going to leave his job, talk to his wife, Emma, about selling their house, and then pack up his life in Canada and join me on a motorcycle adventure around China. It was a journey that would test our endurance – both physical and mental – to its limits, win us a Guinness World Record for the longest continuous journey by motorcycle within a single country, and result in a six-part TV documentary that was aired for the first time in the UK in April 2013 – almost exactly three years after the day Colin and I hatched our crazy plan in Central Park. In fact, it was a journey that would give both of us new perspectives on life, the universe, and pretty much everything.

When we set out from Shanghai in August 2010 – Colin and me on BMW motorcycles, with our cameraman, Chad Ingraham, and a driver following us in a support vehicle – we thought we had some idea of what lay ahead. After a grueling sixty-day, 18,000-kilometer journey that took us to Everest Base Camp, across deserts, and through some of the most isolated regions of China and Tibet, you'd think we'd have learned our lesson. But no: there we were, just a year later, planning our next motorcycle trip – this time, the circumnavigation of India.

It was only *after* we'd done the journey around China that it turned into such a big production. We'd taken Chad along with us to film the whole adventure because I'd had some idea of making a documentary that might be shown on TV. But it wasn't until the journey itself was over that things started to snowball, and that's when we decided to write a book, which was subsequently published under the title *The Middle Kingdom Ride*. However, there was no completed book or TV show when, in October 2011, I told Colin, 'We're going to India.'

Adventures that involve a cameraman, a support vehicle, drivers, food and hotel rooms for at least four people for more than sixty days and nights, as well as many other incidental costs, are expensive. I knew that if our book ever got written and we sold the documentary film we were making to a TV company, the finances would work out. When I broached the idea of going to India to my brother, we were still sitting on a six-figure debt.

After our journey around China, Colin didn't return to Toronto. For the next ten months, he and Emma traveled together around the world before settling in London, where they were making a good life for themselves. Emma had a job she loved and Colin had started studying for an MBA at Hult International Business School. So perhaps I should have predicted my brother's response.

'Are you crazy?' he asked me. 'I don't want to get divorced, and I don't think that the first venture I get involved with as soon as I finish business school should be one that makes no logical business sense at all.'

'It's okay,' I told him, in a voice I hoped conveyed a confident conviction that was almost entirely bogus. 'So we haven't got any funding; but it's the content that really matters. If we wait until we're fully funded, the next trip will never happen.'

'So maybe …!'

I knew I had to head Colin off from what would have been a blind alley of logical argument, commonsense, and caution. 'We'll go next August,' I interrupted him, 'just after you graduate. I've worked it all out. Why would you want to get a job right away when you could do a trip to India first? It's going to be really good. I know it is. Before we go, we can pull together all the strands of *The Middle Kingdom Ride*; then we'll have something to show people that'll have them falling over each other in their eagerness to fund our next great adventure. We're good at this Colin. I *know* we can do it.'

'Well … Okay … I suppose I could talk to Emma and see how she feels about it.' I'd have been happier if there'd been more enthusiasm and less trepidation in his voice. In fact, it would have been good to have been able to detect any enthusiasm at all. But at least he was prepared to consider the idea and hadn't dismissed it out of hand.

I don't know how Colin broached the subject with his wife. I imagine he made a couple of great breakfasts and then chose his moment to tell her, 'Honey, Ryan wants to go to India.' Although he doesn't ever admit it, I suspect he sometimes casts me in the role of 'bad cop'. This time, at least, I couldn't really have argued with him.

Colin and Emma were settled and happy in London, where Colin was planning to start another company when he'd completed his MBA. So perhaps he saw a journey to India as being our last adventure together before he concentrated on building up his new business. For me, it was another part of the evolution of my career as a photographer and film maker. Another motorcycle journey would mean another long separation from my family; fortunately, I think my wife, Jasmine, had already decided that I needed to do whatever I thought I needed I do. Whatever tactic Colin used when he raised the idea with Emma, it clearly worked, and she agreed too.

The problem about choosing to circumnavigate India – or, more accurately, one of the many problems – was that I barely knew it at all. I've lived in China for ten years and before Colin and I set out on the Middle Kingdom Ride, I'd traveled around the country quite extensively on photographic assignments. So I have contacts there, people who know the things I don't know about different areas of the country and can make things happen so that I'm able to get to the places I want to go to. In India, I didn't have a network, and neither did Colin. In fact, in some respects that was a good thing: you can't really call yourself an adventurer if you only ever travel in places you're familiar with – and, having survived the craziness of our journey round China, I was starting to like the idea of a true adventure.

Before Colin and I set out from Shanghai in August 2010, neither of us had any experience of riding motorcycles long distances over difficult terrain – or, in fact, even over easy terrain. I'd done a lot of walking in remote mountain areas, so I did at least have some idea of the limits of my endurance. What I hadn't known then, however, was how far Colin could be pushed before he broke. For that reason, as well as because he's my kid brother, I'd felt a huge sense of responsibility to get him home to his wife in one piece. That was China. Now, as I contemplated our next journey together, I knew just how tough my kid brother really was – both physically and mentally – and that he was more than capable of looking after himself.

In China, I'd wanted Colin to like the things about the country that I like. So, for some of the time at least, I'd been showing him things I'd already seen, although, because you get a different perspective on things when you ride a motorcycle, it turned out that a lot of it was new for me too. Something I particularly liked about the prospect of doing a journey around India was that we'd both be seeing everything for the first time, exploring and discovering the country together and possibly having very different reactions to what we saw and experienced.

Another positive aspect of going somewhere neither of us knew was that this time I wouldn't be the leader, as I'd tended to be in China. Although that was a natural result of my knowledge of the country, I think Colin sometimes got a *bit* fed up with it, which was understandable. This time, I was looking forward to debating and discussing what we were going to do each day, especially in view of the fact that we'd already discovered we work really well together.

Something else we knew from experience by that time was that, as well as adding considerably to the cost, filming really slows you down. We did consider the option of just getting on our motorcycles and going on a trip without all the paraphernalia of film making. Part of me wouldn't mind doing a trip like that; but the truth is that, although I love the adventure, I love the production side of things even more. Having an incredible experience without showing what I've seen to other people so that they can get out there and experience it too would somehow be only half the fun. When some people see something amazing, they seem to be able to absorb it and then move on, whereas I'm looking at it thinking, 'Man, I wish everyone could see what I'm seeing.' I guess that's why I became a documentary photographer. It's also one of the reasons why I can understand what makes social media so addictive. For many people, sharing what they do with their friends and families adds another dimension to it. There's definitely a place for that, particularly when it gets people communicating and connected. The core element of filming the motorcycle journeys I do with my brother is basically the same, because I hope people will see what we've done and think, 'That's awesome. I'm going to do that too.'

The India Ride

Surprisingly, perhaps, after all he'd had to put up with in China, our friend and professional cameraman Chad Ingraham agreed to do it all again and come with us to India. There were several occasions on that first journey when Chad proved himself to be very tough. I guess he thought that, after filming without permits under the ever-present threat of having all the footage he'd shot confiscated – and possibly all of us being arrested – India was going to be a walk in the park by comparison.

There would be the inevitable red tape to be dealt with, of course. I'd decided that this time we'd apply well in advance for all the permits we were going to need to be able to film. That way, there'd be no legal problems hanging over us and we wouldn't have to worry about breaking some rule or regulation we didn't even know existed. That would be a huge plus compared to the situation we'd faced in China, where so many parts of the country are inaccessible and closed to foreigners, if not to Chinese nationals themselves. There were six months from the time the decision was made to go ahead with the India Ride until our planned departure date in August. That meant there'd be plenty of time to sort out all the journalist visas, film-making visas, and permissions we were going to need to enter and film the various temples and other sites we wanted to visit.

We'd had local guides on the Middle Kingdom Ride, and sometimes also drivers who knew the roads in a particular area. This time, I wanted to employ someone Indian as our driver and as secondary cameraman/production assistant to Chad. As we'd be traveling for up to sixty days in what we knew from past experience would often be exhausting and very challenging circumstances, it was going to be really important that everyone involved got on well.

When I asked around, I found a few people who were excited at the idea of doing the film-related part of the job, but none of them was prepared to do the driving. The reason they all gave was pretty much the same: 'Traveling round India in a car would be a bit stressful!' That was when I first started to hear alarm bells ringing, although the sound they were making was muffled by all the 'things to do' that were swirling around in my head like a flock of agitated birds that I was going to deal with one by one.

It was while I was looking for a driver that I first met Daniel Milton. He contacted me to ask if he could interview me for a film project about China he was doing as part of his course at film school in Utrecht. A little while later, he came to my house in Shanghai and we really hit it off. So I offered him the job of film assistant/driver on the spot.

'I'm definitely interested,' he told me. 'But can I have some time to think about it? There are a lot of things I'd need to sort out in Holland before I left.'

To give him an idea of what he might be letting himself in for, I suggested he should watch some TV shows about India, including a BBC program called India on Four Wheels. It was only in retrospect that I realized they didn't give him a very accurate idea of what it was going to be like: it's one thing to make a film with a whole production team, assistants, and drivers, but there'd be no one on the India Ride to take over the driving when the camera was turned off and Dan was tired. So I guess he watched the programs and thought, 'Okay, it looks pretty easy,' because a few days later he contacted me again to say he'd come. He was a welcome addition to the team.

For me, some of the key factors in the decision to go to India were that it's physically beautiful, it has a diversity of landscapes and terrain, and it's one of a handful of countries – others including Russia and Brazil (and China, of course) – that are changing rapidly. From the start, it seemed to be the natural choice. Colin and I were born and raised in Canada, which is the second largest country in the world and has a population of 35 million. There are 1.26 *billion* (1260 million) people in India – that's about 90 million people fewer than there are in China, which is *three times* the size of India. That sort of population density was unimaginable to me. And if you can't imagine something, I believe you need to go and see it.

I've already mentioned that my wife was supportive of what I wanted to do. What she did have reservations about, however, was the fact that going to India wouldn't involve building on what I already knew. 'You're the China guy,' she told me. 'So surely it makes sense to do another program about China?'

She was right, in that there's always something new to discover in China. That's why I love traveling to different parts of the country, taking photographs and finding out about people's lives. But the point was that I didn't really know anything about India. In fact, when the idea first came up, I'd only ever read two books about it – one by Salman Rushdie and the other *Life of Pi* by Yann Martel, which, being a fantasy adventure novel, wasn't a book that was going to provide me with any information that would be either relevant or useful in terms of what we were planning to do. On the other side of the argument, however, was the fact that I enjoy challenging myself, and it seemed to me that India would give me an opportunity to push myself to do more than I thought I could do.

Another positive factor was that English is widely spoken in India, particularly in the towns, which meant that we'd be able to interact with people in a way we hadn't been able to do in China. If you want to put your finger on the pulse of a country and find out about people's lives – how they put food on the table, how they educate their children, and how the changes that are occurring as the old order is overturned affect them on a day-to-day basis – you need to be able to talk to them and to understand

---

[1] The largest country in the world is Russia (17 million km^2); second is Canada (10 million km^2); third is the USA (9.629 million km^2; and a very close fourth is China (9.596 million km^2). The land area of India is just 3 million km^2. (All these figures are approximate.)

what they say to you. While riding through vast expanses of barely populated countryside during the Middle Kingdom Ride, Colin and I had often felt a sense of isolation, which was exacerbated by the fact that when we did encounter people, we couldn't talk to them. Even after all the years I've lived in Shanghai, my Chinese is limited when it comes to having in-depth conversations with local people, who speak many different dialects. And, of course, Colin doesn't speak Chinese at all.

Quite apart from the issue of language, many people in China have a reticence that can quickly become, at best, guarded distrust. It may be an innate characteristic or it may be something they've learned over the generations as a result of the country's sometimes difficult history. It's trite to ascribe 'national characters', I know; but now that I've done it once … I had the impression that Indians tend to be almost the opposite. It was certainly the case that talking to some of the garrulous, friendly people I'd met during earlier brief work visits to a couple of major cities in India had fired my curiosity and made me want to explore the country.

Another plus was that, as well as being home to a significant number of English speakers, India has an established history of tourism, with all the infrastructure that entails. It also has a substantial motorcycle-riding community. In fact, as we were to discover, the attitude of most Indians towards motorcycles and motorcyclists is the antithesis of that in China, where motorcycles are almost always ridden by people who can't afford to buy a car. In India, on the other hand, although many people do ride motorcycles for practical reasons – because they're a relatively affordable form of transport – for many others it's a lifestyle choice. Indians love motorcycles and there's a strong tradition of motorcycle touring in the country, amongst local people as well as visiting foreigners.

There was one major downside to choosing India as the location of our next great adventure: we knew before we went there that it had recently overtaken China to become the country with the highest road-death rate in the world. According to the *Washington Post*, there were 196,000 road deaths in India in 2012. Some statistics that were published in *The Times of India* while we were there were even more shocking: apparently, one in every ten road deaths *throughout the world* occurs in India, as does every sixth car crash worldwide – in a country that has just 1% of all the world's vehicles. Even more astonishingly perhaps, is the fact that the numbers are still rising. We were about to find out why.

Of course, Colin and I did the sensible thing and didn't mention any of the statistics to our families – the fact that we were planning a motorcycle trip on the most dangerous roads in the world was difficult enough to justify to ourselves. Safety was going to have to be our primary concern. I knew from experience that that would mean, amongst other things, not attempting to travel too far each day, because when you get really tired, your concentration level drops, and that's when you have accidents.

Another important safety measure would be for Colin and me to have a really good communication system so that we could talk to each other while we were on our bikes and navigate the traffic together. Maybe two pairs of eyes watching the road and two heads constantly swiveling to try to take in everything that was happening around us would double our chances of staying alive. It was a comforting thought, which made India seem like a reasonable choice after all – until we actually hit the road at the start of our journey and it very abruptly became clear that even doubling our chances still left the odds stacked heavily against our being able to survive for even a few days, let alone several weeks.

The concerns we already had weren't reduced in any way by the fact that, after we'd made the decision to go to India, almost everyone who heard about what we were planning to do seemed to have a story they felt impelled to tell us about someone they knew who'd lost a limb, or worse, while riding a motorcycle in India. There were days when I found it very difficult to believe my own assertion that all we had to do was plan as much as possible in advance and then keep our wits about us while we were on the road.

Fortunately, although it had been my idea to go to India, it wasn't long before Colin was as keen about it as I was. 'At least it can't be any harder than China,' he told me cheerfully. 'We didn't know anything when we set out from Shanghai, but we're experienced now. And this time we'll have permits and visas for film making, so all that side of things will be legal, which is a huge plus.' He laughed as he added, 'Compared to China, circumnavigating India is going to be a breeze.'

'Absolutely,' I said.

Somehow, it didn't seem to be the right moment to tell him I didn't think it was going to be easier at all.

Chapter 2
Setting it up

Ryan ————————————————————————

One of the many important things we'd learned in China was that if you want to stay alive on the roads, it's best to plan things so that you are not riding a motorcycle in the dark. Of course, that isn't always possible: if you're traveling on roads you aren't familiar with, or in traffic that's bad for some reason, if you've had a mechanical problem with your bike, or if something else has gone wrong, even the most carefully laid plans fly out the window. While we were on the Middle Kingdom Ride, we often felt under pressure to cover the daily distances I'd set beforehand, which meant that we'd sometimes push on in circumstances that commonsense was telling us were potentially dangerous. As a result of that experience, I set shorter daily targets for the India Ride. What I didn't know until we hit the road, however, is that it's a lot easier to do 300 km over difficult terrain in China than it is to do even 200 km in the crazy traffic in India.

There were some places that we knew from the outset we wanted to see and some towns we wanted to stay in, so I looked on Google Maps to work out distances and get a rough idea of how long it would take us to get from town A to town B. I guess anyone who knows how to use a computer uses Google Maps when planning any kind of trip; there's no disputing the fact that they're a huge asset. The problem is that, for time and distance planning, they work things out on the basis of, 'It's 153 km from Mumbai to Pune on a new expressway. Traveling at an average speed of around 70-75 kph, it'll take about two hours to go from Hotel A in Mumbai to Hotel B in Pune.' It's a reasonable calculation, if all goes well, and that's probably approximately how long the expressway part of the journey *will* take you. But … what hasn't been factored into the equation are the two hours it'll take you just to get out of Mumbai, and the other hour you'll be driving round Pune in ridiculous traffic trying to find Hotel B. Consequently, the reality is that your journey of 153 km is going to take more like five or six hours. The sun goes down at 6 p.m., so, because you left Mumbai at a time commensurate with the expectation of the journey taking three hours max., you'll be driving into Pune at dusk, when the traffic is even more dangerous than it is at every other time of the day – none of which we knew when we were planning the India Ride.

The journey Colin and I were going to make would begin and end in Delhi and take us around almost the entire periphery of India. As far as I was concerned, working it all out from a distance was the only feasible way of doing it. Circumnavigating

Setting it up

India was going to separate me from my family in Shanghai for at least two months; I didn't want to spend even more time away from home scouting the route. And, quite apart from the time factor, it would have changed everything if I'd already visited the places I wanted to discover for the first time with my brother. So I spent hours at the computer, poring over Google Maps until I'd worked out a route with a timescale so optimistic it would probably have seemed naïve and amusing to anyone with any experience of driving in India.

I went to India for the first time in 2008, on a photographic assignment that involved visiting some hospitals in the south; and I went again a couple of times – to Delhi and Mumbai – during the months when we were planning our journey, to set things up and try to make contact with some potential corporate partners. Colin and I had pretty much funded the Middle Kingdom Ride ourselves and we were planning our trip around India before we'd seen any real financial return on our investment. So it was part of our business strategy to make links with companies that would provide us with financial and/or practical support.

If enthusiasm and belief in the value of what we were doing had been enough to guarantee the kind of funding we needed, I'd have returned to Shanghai from those visits to India with my pockets stuffed full of checks and signed contracts. Unfortunately – and to some extent understandably, I suppose – before they'll part with any cash, company directors want to see concrete proof that they're going to get a good return on their money. Consequently, although everyone I spoke to was genuinely interested in what we were doing in India, the fact that we didn't yet have any firm deal set up with a TV broadcaster for the television series or have a publisher for the book related to our China trip meant that, ultimately, almost all of them responded in the same way:

'So you've made a film that's going to be a TV show. That's great! Soooo ... where is it?'

'It's being edited,' I'd tell them, my heart sinking with the realization that, once again, I'd reached the point in a dialogue when I could have handed them a script that would pretty much recount everything else that was going to be said.

'That's great,' they'd say again, smiling in a way that was intended to convey guarded enthusiasm but that, in reality, merely betrayed their waning interest. 'Soooo ... tell me about the book?'

'We've just started writing it,' I'd say. 'It's going to be great.'

'I'm sure it is.' The people with the money we needed would nod their heads and smile at me again, while I tried to ignore the mocking voice inside my own head that was saying, 'Oh, the book's going to be *great* too is it? At this pivotal moment in the proceedings, you really can't think of any other persuasively descriptive adjective except *great*?'

The truth was that, by that stage, it wouldn't have mattered what I'd said, because they'd already made their decision.

'When you've got signed contracts with a TV broadcaster and a publisher, you make sure you get back in touch with us and we'll talk again,' they'd tell me. Or, sometimes, 'We love what you're doing; unfortunately, this has been a really bad year for us financially ...'

As I say, I suppose you couldn't really blame them – although I did at the time. From their point of view, I was just some hyperbolic, hyperactive Canadian guy who was going to make all sorts of exciting and potentially profitable things happen but who hadn't any proof that he'd actually done so yet. It was disheartening not to be able to make them see what I could see. In the end, despite the fact that lots of people were interested in theory, I didn't manage to raise the sort of money we needed to fund the trip we were planning.

At one stage, someone suggested crowd-funding. It was an interesting idea. For some people, crowd-funding has proved to be a very successful and exciting way of raising money. When I really thought about it though, it didn't seem to be something that was really suitable for an adventure like the one Colin and I were planning. Much as I like the concept of people having the opportunity to become involved in turning someone else's dreams into reality, it didn't seem appropriate to use other people's money to enable us to have adventures and produce TV programs and books. I love sharing my ideas and I hope that, by doing so, I might motivate and inspire someone else to do something they've always dreamed of doing. Ultimately though, I'm expecting to profit financially from what is, in effect, a self-based venture that aims to entertain people – and I don't think entertainment is what crowd-funding is all about.

It began to look as though Colin and I were once again going to be playing the multifaceted and diverse roles of adventure motorcyclists, TV presenters, authors, and financial backers. I really believed it would all come together and that people would be interested in what we were doing. It was a belief it was sometimes hard to hold onto.

There were positives, too, when it came to planning and organizing the India Ride. One of which was the fact that I had more time to set it up than I'd had before our circumnavigation of China. When we set out from Shanghai in August 2010, we didn't really know what we were doing; we certainly didn't know whether it would all work out okay or prove to be a total disaster. This time, at least I had some experience on which to base all the decisions that needed to be made.

Colin and I weren't the only ones who were nervous and uncertain about it all: our families had their own, very significant, doubts too. It wasn't really until they'd seen the film footage of the Middle Kingdom Ride that they began to understand there was a real point to what we were doing. Then their attitude tended to be, 'I guess, if you survived China, there was always

Setting it up

going to be a part two. So go ahead. Just be really careful and don't get yourselves killed.' So at least in that sense the build-up to the India Ride was less stressful. But there were still all the other stresses associated with what sometimes seemed to be an infinite list of decisions that had to be made and of things that had to be planned, organized, ordered, and bought.

When preparing for any kind of fairly large-scale journey, you reach a point when, on the one hand, you wish you had more time to do everything that needs to be done and, on the other, you want it all to be over and would almost be happy to set out the next day, ready or not. Then, suddenly, the day of your departure arrives.

Our cameraman, Chad, also lives in Shanghai and he and I flew out together to Delhi on the 21st of August 2012, eleven days before we were due to set off on the India Ride. Four days after Chad and I got there, Colin flew in from London, and then Daniel arrived from Utrecht. Despite weeks of preparation – which had had to be fitted in around all the many other aspects of our more routine daily lives – there were still a lot of strands that needed to be pulled together. And as well as all the practical things we had to do, we wanted some time to acclimatize to India, to see at least some of the city, visit the Jama Masjid in Old Delhi, which is the largest mosque in India, and do some filming that would set the scene for our now-imminent adventure.

I really enjoyed those days in Delhi. As soon as our plane

touched down, what we were about to do finally became real: I was setting out on another adventure with my brother, during which anything could happen. I could feel the excitement building up inside me. People who know me well might say that I'm borderline hyperactive. It's certainly true that I don't 'do' relaxing; I don't think I've ever sat back in an armchair and read a newspaper, for example. I need to be *doing* things all the time. And as there was plenty that had to be done in the days before we left Delhi, I was in my element.

There was one less positive aspect of spending those few days in Delhi before our departure, which was that as we crisscrossed the city in taxis doing the last few things that needed to be done, we found ourselves right in the middle of all the crazy stuff taking place on the roads. It was probably even more shocking for Colin than it was for me, not least because his very abrupt introduction to the streets of Delhi on the day he arrived from London included seeing a motorcyclist hit a cow. The motorcycle seemed to explode on impact and the guy flew up into the air like a human cannonball, before landing on the other side of 1000 lb of impassive, apparently impervious beef.

We knew, of course, that cows are sacred to Hindus. What we hadn't really understood was that, as a consequence, they're allowed to wander unrestrained throughout the country. What that actually means is that they can meander across city streets or stand, impervious and indifferent, in the middle of a road

soon be leaving the city behind us and traveling on roads that would be considerably less dangerous. It was a misconception born of ignorance!

Once we'd arrived in Delhi, there was still some shopping to be done. We'd decided not to eat any meat while we were traveling, in the hope of avoiding food poisoning and debilitating sickness. In addition to all the tales of horrific accidents, it seemed that everyone we spoke to while we were planning the trip had a horror story about the terrible sickness they or someone they knew had suffered as a result of eating meat in India. Even allowing for the 'traveler's tale' aspect of what they said, it seemed sensible not to take the risk. However, we knew we might also need a plan B; so we went to a pharmacy and bought a range of anti-sickness pills. Next, we went to an electronics store, where we bought mobile phones, local SIM cards, and cards that would enable us to connect to the Internet via our laptops in hotels that didn't have any form of internet access – which we knew would be the case in several of them.

Apart from shopping, one of the other main events that took place during those days in Delhi was picking up our SUV support vehicle from the Mahindra dealership. A handing-over ceremony had been arranged and after we'd signed all the necessary paperwork, one of the guys from Mahindra gave a short speech. Then they took us outside, where they pulled a big red tarpaulin off one of the company's tiger-stripe-painted promotional cars. A young woman drew a Hindu symbol on the vehicle and then Colin and I broke a coconut, in a ritual that's performed at the start of all new ventures to dispose of any negative energy that might hinder their progress.

Daniel had arrived in Delhi that day, and as he was the one who was going to be at the wheel of the SUV for the next seven or eight weeks – with Chad and his camera in the passenger seat beside him – it seemed logical for him to drive it back to the hotel after the ceremony. On the other hand, I decided, it was probably best not to risk freaking him out so soon; so I drove. In fact, it was the first time I'd ever been in the driving seat of a vehicle in Delhi and it was one of the most nerve-racking journeys of my entire life. During the hour it took us to drive the relatively short distance from the dealership to our hotel, I think the only word Daniel said was 'Shit!' Clearly, my plan to protect him from being freaked out had failed.

The second big event during those days of preparation in Delhi was picking up our motorcycles from Manzil Motors, a Royal Enfield dealership. After the owner, who was a really nice guy and a keen motorcycle rider called Puneet Gaur, had sold us our motorcycles, we spent some time with his mechanics, who showed us how to do oil changes and how to fix some of the minor problems that might occur.

One of the main reasons for choosing the Royal Enfield Thunderbird 350cc was that it's made in India. The BMWs we'd ridden in China were great, although expensive, particularly by the time we'd paid the 100% luxury tax levied on all non-essential goods imported into the country. The problem on the Middle Kingdom Ride had been that few people in China know how to fix BMW motorcycles, which meant that when we broke a clutch, we ended up being delayed for days while we waited for parts to be brought in from abroad, all of which added even more to the already considerable costs of the journey. So, this time, we'd chosen a make of bike that is widely available and ridden in India, that we assumed could be easily fixed if we broke down, and that, incidentally and fortuitously, cost a fraction of what we'd paid for the BMWs.

Even though the model we chose wasn't a specialist off-road bike, its retail price, of $2500, is way above what the majority of people in India can afford. So people were interested when they saw us on the road, which led to a lot of interactions we might otherwise not have had.

In fact, the bikes turned out to be a good choice for several reasons: as well as generating a lot of conversations with local people, they were, as predicted, easy to fix, light, and suitable for the Indian terrain. We thought they'd be safer too, because they don't do more than about 80 kph flat out. However, as we were soon to discover, it wasn't the capacity of the bikes that was going to limit our speed; the crazy car, truck and bus drivers, the cyclists, kids, and livestock are what create potentially lethal havoc on almost every road throughout the country.

After we'd got the SUV and the bikes, we picked up our motorcycle gear. One of the sponsors we'd managed to get on board for the India Ride was a Dutch-based company called REV'IT!, which provided us with all the motorcycle and casual clothing we were going to need, including jackets, boots, gloves, T-shirts etc. During one of my two previous visits to India, I'd met a really nice guy, called Jasjiv Saluja, who owned a motorcycle-clothing shop, and I'd arranged for REV'IT! to ship everything to his store.

Next, we went to a barber's shop to get our faces shaved for what would be the last time until we returned to Delhi at the end of our journey. And then we visited a fortune teller. Belief in the existence of some higher power is widely held in India – whether it be one god or several, or some sort of astrology-based mysticism. It was the latter that our guy was into. First, he asked about our star signs, significant dates and numbers; then he told us which days during the next couple of months would be good for us in various ways, and which would be bad.

'No real danger lies ahead of you,' he said. 'Your journey will be financially successful.' Both statements were good news. And then came the bad: 'The day you are planning to leave is a Saturday as well as the first day of the month. This is not a good day to start a trip. You should wait until the next day.'

Although we were reassured to know that any dangers

we were going to encounter were likely to be minor and that the financial side of things was going to work out, we chose to ignore the bad news and not postpone our departure as advised: sometimes, pragmatism rules.

We'd arrived in India without any real preconceptions about what it was going to be like. Although we knew that Delhi wasn't necessarily a microcosmic representation of the rest of the country, it certainly gave us a very definite and lasting first impression. It's a city that teems with life: every street is crammed almost to bursting point with people – in vehicles and on them, as well as on foot – and with stray animals, many of which would only be found in farmyards in most other countries. What struck us even more forcefully than the swirling mass of life on the streets, however, was the total, unrelieved chaos of it all. I suppose that's what happens in the absence of any kind of organization: pandemonium fills the void.

Many of the streets of Delhi are unlit; where street lights have been installed, some of them are broken – or maybe they never worked at all. There seem to be very few policemen and a very large number of roundabouts. Unfortunately, as every road user is apparently be marching to the beat of his own, peculiar, drum, the roundabouts fail to assist the flow of traffic in any way. Instead, they become a focus for traffic jams, which in turn fuel the already high levels of frustration and add to the constant cacophony of car horns.

In the few days we were in Delhi, we saw more road accidents than most people in the West would see over the course of several years, which didn't do much to help the process of trying to psyche ourselves up for the long journey that lay ahead. And, as well as being chaotic and unnerving, the city was also incredibly hot, with temperatures reaching at least 40 °C every day while we were there.

'It'll be better when we get out of the urban area and onto the open road,' we kept telling each other.

Despite everything I've said above, I don't want to make it sound as though our first impressions of India were all negative. It's true that we were daunted – in fact, almost overwhelmed – by the noise, the lack of order and organization, the extraordinary number of people, and the massive volume of traffic. Although, in some ways, I appreciated the raw energy of Delhi, its many excesses weren't like anything any of us had ever experienced before: being there was like being under siege in a city that had fallen prey to anarchy. But there were two huge positives that quickly became apparent: the people are incredibly friendly and they were interested in what we were doing.

The sense that local people were supportive and wanted us to succeed was a motivating force for us, and very much in contrast to the way things had been in China, where we'd felt the need to be secretive and not let anyone know what we were planning to do. That sense that people were rooting for us was to stay with us throughout our journey around India and, on several occasions, it was to provide a very much-needed boost to our flagging morale. Sometimes, when your 'inner strength' has been substantially depleted, the goodwill and smiling encouragement of other people can lift your spirits and help to get you through a really tough day.

A couple of days before we were due to set out on the India Ride, we were invited by Sanjay Sharma, the manager of the hotel we were staying in, to ride out and meet him and some of his friends for lunch at a town called Sohna.

'It's about 60 kilometers southwest of Delhi,' Sanjay told us. 'It'll be like a test ride – it'll give you a chance to make sure everything's working well on your motorcycles.'

It certainly seemed like a good idea. We estimated that the drive would take us about an hour, which would allow Colin and me to test the bikes, the cameras, and the communication system in our helmets, and give Daniel the opportunity to drive the SUV on roads outside the city. What could go wrong?

We set out from Delhi at 11 a.m. in incredible heat wearing our motorcycle gear and helmets, and within minutes we were cooked. When I'd asked Sanjay what the main road from Delhi to Sohna was like, he'd said 'So-so'. I guess it all depends on what you're used to. We'd have categorized it as 'appalling'.

It took us two and a half hours to drive 60 km over a scant, incomplete layer of tarmac, which disappeared altogether at frequent and irregular intervals, to be replaced by huge, water-filled potholes that came at least halfway up the wheels on our motorcycles. Having spent the last ten years living in China, what was particularly surprising to me was the fact that this was the main road between Delhi and what was clearly intended to be the high-class rural resort of Sohna. In China, they'd have built a good road first, as part of the overall investment and to enable people from the city to get to the resort as quickly and easily as possible. Without a decent road, although the place itself might be amazing, why would anyone go to all the hassle of getting there?

Another aspect of that day that shocked all of us was the terrible poverty we saw in some of the rural villages we drove through. There's poverty in China, of course, but you get the sense there that people are trying to improve their lives – even if, in many cases, that means moving out of the countryside into the cities to find work. En route to Sohna that day, we witnessed for the first time something that was to become very apparent to us later – the fact that the poverty in India is on a completely different scale from that in China, or from anywhere else I've ever been, and that people seem simply to accept it, perhaps for cultural or religious reasons. Over the next few weeks, poverty and the passive acceptance of it by a vast number of people became recurring themes of the India Ride.

When we finally arrived at the Westin Hotel in Sohna, almost two hours later than scheduled, everyone was very welcoming and friendly and we had a good lunch. Then we left to drive back to Delhi in heavy traffic and gathering darkness.

Before our visit to Sohna, we'd felt excited about what lay ahead for us. After it, some of our confidence seemed to have evaporated. What we didn't know at the time, however, was that the main road from Delhi to Sohna was probably one of the worst roads we were going to encounter throughout the entire trip. Over the last few days, we'd sat in taxis with our hands over our faces and made jokes – at least partly to try to release some of our nervous anxiety – about being at the mercy of apparently manic taxi drivers as they forged erratic and potentially lethal paths through the crowded streets. Now, as the day of our departure loomed, I think we were all having second thoughts about the reality of what we'd let ourselves in for.

On the upside, our SUV had been blessed and a fortune teller had predicted financial success and few real dangers. After our venture was further blessed by a priest in a Hindu ceremony called a Puja, we almost managed to convince ourselves that we were invincible.

Chapter 3
Day one

Colin ────────────────────────────

Is there some unspoken law of the universe, which states that the first day of every journey of any significant extent will be the hardest day of the entire trip?

On our last night in Delhi, we double-checked to make sure we'd packed everything we were going to need for the next sixty days, ordered in pizzas, and then Ryan, Chad, Dan, and I sat together in the hotel watching the newly edited footage of what would become a three-hour TV series called *The Middle Kingdom Ride.* I think watching it ramped up the excitement for all of us. For Ryan, particularly, it was also a reminder that the next few weeks weren't just going to be about riding motorcycles around India: by the time we returned to Delhi at the end of our journey, we had to have some equally good footage of our new adventure.

We were awake by 5 o'clock on the morning of Saturday 1st September 2012. Half an hour later, we set out from the hotel and drove through the dark, eerily empty streets of the city. In fact, that wasn't exactly the way it happened: once everything was loaded into the SUV and we were ready to leave, we spent the best part of ten minutes trying to start the bikes. When we'd taken them on a test ride the day before, everything had seemed to be working well. Now, at the crucial moment, when we were anxious to get going before the streets of Delhi became a crazy, hooting mess of morning traffic, the engines simply wouldn't fire up. It was almost as if they were out of fuel, which we knew wasn't the case. It didn't make sense that both bikes apparently had exactly the same problem. But there we were, all ready to go and unable to start the bikes, our frustration mounting with every dull click of the ignition.

Eventually, it was one of the guys who worked at the hotel who solved the problem. Smiling nervously, as though anxious not to cause offence, he told us. 'You have to turn the switch.' When we both stared at him blankly, he stepped forward, reached out his hand to flip a switch, first on my bike, then on Ryan's, and said, 'Now try.' This time, the bikes roared into life. I guess everyone had assumed we knew that you're supposed to turn off the fuel supply to the engine when you park up your bike; someone must have done it for us the previous day. It was all part of the learning curve!

We'd decided to start our journey at the India Gate, an impressive stone memorial in the heart of New Delhi that was designed by the British architect Sir Edwin Lutyens and commemorates the tens of thousands of Indian soldiers who were killed in the First World War and the Third Afghan War in 1919. We were met there by Sanjay Sharma, the general manager of the Westin Hotel, and two of his friends, who were keen motorcyclists and who had offered to drive with us out of the city to have breakfast. They wanted to take us to Murthal, a village about 50 km north of Delhi on National Highway 1 that's renowned for its little restaurants, called dhabas, which line the sides of the road.

In fact, the place where we ate that morning looked more like a truck stop or a gas station than a restaurant. There were tables and chairs under a red tin roof beside the road, and another seating area inside, next to the kitchen. When we arrived, at about 7.30 a.m., it was already full. Some young motorcyclists and a group of scruffy, bearded students who were traveling together in a dilapidated-looking bus wanted to know what we were doing and where we were going. Their enthusiasm when we told them about the India Ride was infectious and I began to feel excited again about the adventure we'd just embarked on. Despite the makeshift appearance of the restaurant, the food was excellent, and after a breakfast of freshly baked bread and yoghurt washed down with piping hot tea, we were ready to hit the road.

Our destination on day 1 was Shimla, a town in the mountains about 400 km north of Delhi that is a popular tourist destination, particularly during the summer months, when people go there to escape the stifling temperature in the city. By the time we set off from Murthal, the heat was already intense and within minutes I felt as though I was being boiled alive in my motorcycle gear. It was near the end of the monsoon season and we knew that when it started to rain – as it had done for an hour or more every day while we were in Delhi – the dust that covered the road would turn to mud, and then we'd have no chance of reaching Shimla before dusk. There was no rain that day, however; just unremitting heat, sweat, and dirt.

National Highway 1, which is the main road running due north from Delhi, has two or three lanes in either direction, divided by a central barrier, so it was relatively safe to do 80 kph on the motorcycles – which is pretty much their top speed. By about 2 p.m., we'd reached Chandigarh, where we stopped in the shade at the side of the road to drink some water. There was about another 100 km to go before we'd reach Shimla, but we'd come to the end of the highway. From that point on, the road would twist and turn through the mountains, so there was no way of knowing how long the last stretch of the day's journey would take us.

After talking to Chad and Daniel, we decided to push on – at least we'd be off the busy highway and driving through the mountains on quieter roads, and even if we only averaged 25 kph, we'd still reach Shimla before dusk, which was at around

6 p.m. Before making the decision, we'd considered all the known factors and all the probabilities based on our own past experience and on intelligent assumption. The problem was: we assumed that the mountain road would be 'quiet' compared to the highway, whereas I doubt that there's a single 'quiet' road in the whole of India. Even in the mountains, there are small villages at least every 5 km and larger ones every 10. Between the villages, there are houses at the sides of the roads; and in the villages there are adults, children, dogs, goats, cows, donkeys, people on scooters and bicycles, carts pulled by people and animals, trucks, and tuk-tuks that stop abruptly, repeatedly, and without any warning. All of which means that not only do you have to drive really slowly in the immediate vicinity of the villages themselves, but also that you can't go much faster on the more open stretches of road, for fear of hitting the human beings and livestock that are wandering beside and across it with what appears to be a complete and total lack of any concept of danger.

For the next five hours, we drove at a maximum speed of 20 kph, and for most of that time we were stuck behind other vehicles, trying not to ingest more than was unavoidable of the filthy black fumes that spewed out of every truck. Ryan and I could have overtaken the crawling traffic on our bikes, but that would have meant leaving Chad and Daniel in the SUV far behind us, which was something we'd decided we wouldn't do: if anything interesting were to happen, we didn't want Chad and his camera to be a couple of kilometers back down the road. It was a decision that it was sometimes hard to stick to, because the heat, the fumes, and the risk of hitting something or someone were constant and exhausting.

For me though, there was *something* to mitigate the otherwise almost completely negative aspects of the day's ride – the monkeys. There were little orange-colored monkeys everywhere, sitting at the sides of the road, on buildings and in trees, watching the chaotic world go by, or suddenly darting across in front of the oncoming traffic, having apparently remembered something they needed to do. I was enthralled by them. While we were riding, Ryan and I talked to each other almost continuously on the intercom systems in our helmets, and I think he got a bit tired of my saying, 'Check out that one. And look at that one – she's got a tiny baby clinging on underneath her.' Maybe the heat and the chaos of the road were getting to him, or maybe it was the fact that he's seen enough monkeys in China not to be as fascinated by them as I was, that caused him eventually to say, with exasperated terseness, 'Yeah, Colin. I see them. What? Have you never been to a zoo before?' I decided not to point out that *these* monkeys were wild.

Despite the wildlife, the unpredictable pedestrians, capricious cyclists, and dangerously overconfident drivers of all the other vehicles on the road, we did make it to Shimla that day. We arrived there at seven o'clock and checked into a horrible hotel.

Day one

For reasons of cost, we always tried to stay two people to a room, but the hotel in Shimla had only four single rooms, each of which contained a damp bed, a DIY shower that basically consisted of a bucket and a spoon, a very nasty bath tub, an even nastier toilet, and, in the case of my room, a discarded condom wrapper. We were exhausted; all we wanted was to have a shower in a clean bathroom, eat, and then fall asleep in a comfortable bed, which made finding ourselves in a hotel like that even more disheartening than it might otherwise have been. It wasn't a great start to our journey.

We were paying what, in India, amounted to a fairly substantial price for those rooms, certainly enough to expect there to be soap and shampoo in the bathroom. So I was irritated when I had to call down to reception to ask for some. A few minutes later, I was standing butt naked in the shower, trying to wash off the day's grime by ladling cold water from a bucket over my head, when I heard the bedroom door open. Before I'd had a chance to react, a guy walked into the bathroom and handed me some soap!

When I was at Ryerson University in Toronto, I worked for a few summers on the front desk of a hotel, where there was a strict procedure that had to be followed before you entered any of the rooms. Even if you were fairly certain that a room was empty, you'd knock three times on the door and call out 'Hello'. If there was no answer, you put your key in the lock, opened the door just a little bit, and said, 'Is there anyone there? I'm coming in.' If you'd waltzed into a room when there was a guest in it – let alone into the bathroom when someone was in the shower – you'd probably have been fired and the guest would have ended up staying at the hotel free of charge, at the very least. I guess, when you live in a densely populated country like India, you grow up without any sense of personal space – your own or other people's.

Fortunately, the hotel in Shimla turned out to be the most expensive and the worst of our entire trip. The problem was, we didn't know that at the time, and we began to wonder what lay ahead for us in all the other towns where we'd be staying.

Surprisingly perhaps, we had a good meal at the hotel on that first night. It was simpler to eat at the hotels we stayed at, which is what we ended up doing almost every night throughout the trip. (Chad always ordered our dinners for us, and we had some great meals – all of them vegetarian.) It meant we didn't have as much interaction with local people as we'd have liked to have. But we were almost invariably exhausted when we stopped for the night, and having to go out to look for somewhere to eat would have seemed like an additional and sometimes insurmountable hurdle.

It hadn't taken long that morning before my body began to ache. Every time we stopped, I could barely swing my leg back over the seat or raise my arms to the handlebars because of the incredible pain in muscles I hadn't used since Ryan and

Day one

I had circumnavigated China a couple of years earlier. Riding a motorcycle seems to involve using muscles that are latent during all other activities, even including all the sporting activities Ryan and I get involved in to try to keep ourselves fit. By the end of day 1, my back was sore, my arms were throbbing, my ankles were stiff, and – as even ten hours of solid riding hadn't succeeded in molding the seat of the motorcycle to the shape of my butt – I had a severe pain in my ass. The muscles in my fingers were burning too, and although I'd exercised my hands as much as possible during the month before we'd set out on the India Ride, nothing can really prepare you for having to clasp the clutch for ten hours straight.

It was the tingling in my legs that kept me awake that night though. When you've fallen into bed too tired even to care about the dirty, damp sheets and you're still wide awake at 3 a.m., you start imagining all sorts of things. As the minutes ticked by – ridiculously slowly – and, despite being totally exhausted, I was unable to fall asleep, I could feel myself starting to panic. What was going on? What would cause my legs to be numb and uncomfortable? Did I have a blood clot? Should I get up and do something about it before it traveled from my legs to my chest? Or would the act of getting up itself precipitate the movement of the clot and result in my untimely death in a filthy hotel room in Shimla when our journey had barely begun? (This might be difficult to believe in view of the above, but I'm actually the brother who doesn't dramatize!)

In fact, the answer to all those questions was simple and obvious; I was just too fatigued to think of it: for the first time in two years, I'd spent ten hours sitting in one position on a motorcycle wearing tight boots. It would have been surprising if my legs hadn't ached.

Prior to setting out on a long journey, everything is unknown. You've looked at maps and tried to work out how far you'll be able to travel in six or eight hours, but until your tires actually hit the tarmac, it's all just theory. Clearly, hoping to do 400 km on the first day had been too ambitious. We should have known that day 1 would be difficult. Before we went to bed that night, Ryan and I compared our aches and pains and joked that, on our next trip, we'll get up on day 1 at 7 a.m., have a leisurely breakfast and a latte, ride until noon, check into a nice hotel with a pool just in time for a cocktail before lunch, and spend the afternoon relaxing.

As I lay in bed that night, desperate to fall sleep and trying not to think about what might be ahead for us during the next sixty days, I comforted myself with the thought that at least we'd ended the day where we'd hoped to be and we'd arrived there safely.

Day 1 was over. Day 2 was going to be a breeze by comparison.

Chapter 4
Paragliding at Manali

Ryan ────────────────────────────────

From Shimla, we traveled north to Manali. We'd expected the roads to take us through empty, mountainous landscapes, but once again they were congested. There were people almost everywhere you looked, in vehicles and on foot. Once again, we'd been overambitious in our estimation of how far we'd be able to travel in one day and when we finally arrived at Manali, we ended up spending 40 minutes going round in circles looking for our hotel in the dark. It was only day 2, and already we'd broken our golden rule about not riding at night. Perhaps it was a timely lesson, because it was an experience that scared us enough to make us swear never to do it again.

'When you're setting out to circumnavigate a country the size of India, isn't it a bit embarrassing to have to admit to being unable to find your way round a town in the dark?' I hear you ask. And I can understand why you might raise that question. All I can say in answer to it is that, with bad instructions, substandard mapping, an incomplete address for the hotel, unmade roads, and inadequate, sometimes totally absent, signage and street lighting, not to mention the fact that we'd just driven 350 km on congested roads, the whole thing becomes a nightmare. It taught us one thing though: only stay in hotels that have websites, because if a hotel has a website, you can usually find it on Google Maps – although even that didn't ever guarantee we'd be able to do locate it on our sat navs.

Another thing we were reminded of on day 2 was that when we had long distances to cover, it was better not to stop for lunch. Eating in the middle of the day left us feeling bloated and sleepy, and once you've lost your edge, it's very hard to get it back. What we needed to do when we got on the bikes every morning was switch into 'war mode' and stop only occasionally, and briefly, to eat biscuits and drink water.

The next day was a rest day – or, more accurately perhaps, an off-bike day, because on the days when we weren't traveling, we didn't really *rest* at all. It might seem odd to have scheduled a rest day after just two days on the road. The reason I'd done it had nothing to do with taking a relaxing break: Manali is the extreme sports capital of India. Whatever high-risk activity appeals to you, be it rock climbing, whitewater rafting, heli-skiing, base jumping … you can do it all at Manali. In an attempt to try to scare ourselves to death, we had chosen paragliding.

When we woke up on the morning of day 3, it was pouring with rain. I rang the guy at the Himalayan Extreme Adventure

Center to find out what the plan was and he told me cheerfully, 'Obviously you can't jump in the rain. But don't worry; it'll clear. Come to the office and we'll work it out.'

The four of us drove in the SUV to the adventure center, where we were met by Daglas, the guy who was going to drive us the rest of the way to the base of the mountain where the death-defying event would take place, weather permitting. He was as upbeat about it all as his colleague had been on the phone and he repeated the assurance that, 'It'll be fine. The rain will have cleared by the time we get there.' So we piled into his vehicle for the half-hour drive to the foot of the mountain, which was a journey that turned out to be one of the worst experiences any of us had ever had in a car. The road was bad, the guy's driving was horrible, and we were all car sick. And he was wrong about the weather: it was still raining when we arrived at the mountain.

Having almost fallen over each other in our haste to get out of the car, we stood around for 40 minutes until Daglas shrugged his shoulders and said, 'Okay, so not today.' It was disappointing, particularly because we'd only be in Manali for one day, so couldn't simply reschedule. What was even worse than the disappointment, however, was the prospect of having to get back into the car and endure another half an hour of being driven at speed along a terrible road by a cheerfully reckless and apparently fearless driver.

The guy tugged and jerked at the steering wheel and swerved, too fast, around blind corners on the narrow road without even touching the brake. As he bumped and crashed through potholes, we tried, mostly unsuccessfully, to protect our heads from being smashed repeatedly against the sides and roof of the vehicle. At least it gave us something to focus on other than the churning sickness in our stomachs. It was raining even harder by that time, and as the vehicle didn't have any functioning windscreen wipers, the guy couldn't see much of the road ahead, which didn't seem to bother him at all.

When he pulled up outside the office, he jumped out of the car and said, 'Wait till four o'clock. If the rain hasn't cleared by then, I'll call by the hotel and return your money.'

Sitting around waiting for something that was beginning to seem very unlikely to happen wasn't the way we'd wanted to spend our day in Manali, but there wasn't any alternative. On the positive side, at least we'd arrived back at the hotel without sustaining any serious injuries, other than some cranial bruising!

We ordered lunch and were sitting eating it disconsolately when the rain suddenly stopped and the sun burst through the clouds. Within five minutes, Daglas was on the phone. 'I'm coming to pick you up,' he said. 'We're going back.'

Our flagging spirits lifted immediately at the thought that we were going to get the chance to paraglide after all. And then they sank again as we realized that, first, we had to survive another horrible journey to the mountain. The good news – if you really looked for it – was that jumping off a mountain strapped to a parachute couldn't be any more dangerous than sitting in the back of an SUV that was being driven by a fatalistic maniac on a terrible road.

This time we were met at the foot of the mountain by two of Daglas's buddies who were going to be jumping with us. When Colin and I went together to the launch site in the cable car, it became clear we'd been asking ourselves the same questions. Who are these guys? Are they licensed to do this? Do you even need a license to take people paragliding in India, where, in so many spheres of life, it seems that anything goes? Why do their harnesses and backpacks – which contained the parachutes from which we would soon be suspended a couple of hundred feet above the rocks – look so ... raggedy?

Again, if you looked for it with enough determination, there was a bright side, of sorts, in that any worries we'd had about the wisdom of what we were about to do were subjugated by more urgent concerns related to the infrastructure of it all. Was this really what we wanted to be doing? Three days into an epic motorcycle journey around India, with all the costs and promises that involved, did we really want to risk everything by leaping off the side of a mountain strapped to some apparently super-laid-back guys, about whom we knew nothing, who in turn would be strapped to a bit of material? It was a question that didn't really need to be asked: for anyone with any sense at all, the answer had to be 'No!'

On the other hand, there was the film to consider: paragliding was bound to provide us with some good footage – and the show *must* go on.

Colin and I wore our own motorcycle jackets and helmets to do the jump, so that we could make use of the integral audio and cameras. Chad went first, filming his own descent, so that he'd be on the ground to film Colin's, then mine, and finally Daniel's.

'How long have you been doing this?' I asked Daglas as I waited my turn to jump.

'About three years.' It was not a very reassuring answer.

'Oh right,' I said. 'So … you've done it a whole bunch of times.'

'Oh yeah.' He nodded his head and smiled. 'At least ten times.'

In reality, the guy's a pro; he's done the jump hundreds of times, and so have his buddies who jumped with us. But, even though I knew he was joking, I don't think my laughter was entirely convincing.

When Colin told his wife, Emma, that we were planning to go paragliding, she asked him, 'Why would you want to do something dangerous on top of something dangerous?' It was a reasonable question, which we were to ask ourselves repeatedly throughout the India Ride. The motorcycle journey itself was hazardous for many reasons. (In fact, our wives would have had even graver concerns for our safety than they already had if they'd known what the roads in India were really like.) So why, indeed, would we want to compound the risks still further by jumping off a mountain? The truth was that although the question *was* reasonable, it was one for which we didn't have any satisfactory answer.

All too soon, it was my turn to jump. The pro who's strapped to your back has to have an unimpeded view when you're in the air, which means that your head has to be at his chest level while you're running before 'take-off'. So you're carrying the weight of a fully grown man, who's shouting in your ear, 'Go, go, go! Run! Run!' If your adrenalin isn't already pumping, it's certainly flooding your entire body by the time you start to pound across the uneven rocky soil towards the edge of the mountain.

It had already been explained to me that, 'As soon as you start running, you're 100% committed to jumping off the mountain. At the moment when you launch yourself off the side, your chute has to be at a 45° angle. If you stop running, it won't catch the wind; and if it doesn't catch the wind, you're going to fall.'

As the person in front, I was the one who had to set the pace, and as I ran towards the precipice with every muscle in my body straining, the guy's words were echoing in my head: 'Once you start running, don't stop, whatever happens. At that point, everything depends on you.'

There wasn't a single aspect of the experience that wasn't scary and, in addition to a thudding heart, I had an acutely painful groin. I hadn't managed to adjust my harness properly before the first shouted instruction to 'Run!' and, as well as being incredibly tight, it was cutting into me in some very tender places. You're supposed to *sit* in the harness, not hang in it lopsidedly, like I was doing. But once I'd started to run, there was no time to do anything about it. Suddenly, the wind caught our sail and we were swept off the mountain by a rising column of air.

By the time we were drifting across the sky, high above the floor of the valley, there was no way I was going to start grappling with clasps and trying to loosen the harness. The whole escapade was already perilous enough without bringing into the equation the additional risk of unbuckling the wrong clasp and plummeting, in unharnessed freefall, 200 feet to the ground below. Later, when I had both of my own feet firmly on the ground and was in a position to be able to reflect more calmly on our paragliding adventure, I realized that the outcome I'd imagined probably wasn't possible: I guess the kit has to be pretty much idiot-proof. While we were airborne, however, it didn't seem like a good time to put it to the test.

Of course, Daglas wasn't aware of the problem with my harness, and as we glided along the curve of the mountainside, he kept shouting in my ear, 'Sit back!' I tried to tell him I couldn't – not least because I didn't know *how* to – but I don't think he could hear me.

Colin had landed quite heavily, so although I wasn't keen to prolong the airborne bit, I wasn't much looking forward to touchdown either. Fortunately, we came down in mud and the padded motorcycle pants helped soften the impact. We'd only been in the air for about five minutes, but, believe me, when you're wishing you were almost anywhere else, doing almost anything else, and your personal bits feel as though they're being crushed in a persistently tightening vice, five minutes is a very long time.

I admit that the whole paragliding thing wasn't an overly well-thought-out idea. There are moments in your life when every brain cell and every fiber of your being is screaming at you not to do something. For me, running off the side of a mountain strapped to a man and a parachute was one of those moments. It was only afterwards that we really allowed ourselves to think about the long list of things that could have gone horribly wrong. High on that list was the very real risk of one of us breaking an ankle, wrist, arm, or leg three days into a sixty-day motorcycle journey that had involved months of planning and preparation, not to mention the investment of a considerable sum of money. I'd just like to say in my defense that it seemed like a good idea at the time, particularly as it wasn't something any of us was ever going to do again. And Chad did get some great film footage.

Daniel had been the least keen of all of us to do the jump, and I don't think the reality of the experience did anything to change his mind. Despite his very rational misgivings, he did it though, maybe only because we'd agreed at the outset that if one of us was going to do it, we all were – just as we agreed afterwards that we would all never do it again. It was scary, counterintuitive, and stressful at the time, but it was pretty cool in retrospect. And, luckily, we all survived it.

That night, as we were eating our dinner at the hotel, we got talking to some motorcycle tourists who were sitting at the table next to ours and who were heading out the following morning on the road to Leh, the ancient capital of the Himalayan kingdom of Ladakh. We'd wanted to travel north from Manali to Leh too, and from there to the Khardung La Pass on the old caravan route to Kashgar. Leh itself is a popular tourist destination, but because Colin and I had journalist rather than tourist visas, our application to visit the northern border areas of India had been refused. The reason we were given was that, in the light of recent terrorist attacks in the largely Muslim area of Srinagar, it would be unwise for us to take the risk – which was ironic, considering what we'd been doing that day.

In fact, there were very few red-tape moments in India – particularly compared to our experience in China; but that was one of them. It was the price we had to pay for sticking to the rules and doing everything the 'right' way. Our disappointment at not being able to do some tough riding along the highest road in the world was compounded by the excited anticipation of the guys we talked to that night. All I could do was try to comfort myself with the thought that there'd be plenty of other adventures during the coming days to keep the adrenalin pumping.

Chapter 5
The Saach Pass

Colin ─────────────────────────

Unable to travel north to Leh, we headed west from Manali on day 4, then south into the province of Himachal Pradesh and through the Saach Pass, which connects the Chamba and Pangi valleys in the Pir Ranjal Range of the Himalayas. It isn't much of a road; in fact, it's more like a narrow, unmetaled track that climbs to a height of 4420 m above sea level and is only open between the months of June/July and October each year.

I think at least part of the reason why Ryan chose that route after we'd been refused visas to travel to Leh and then on through the Khardung La Pass was because it was the most ridiculous road on the map: he was determined that, one way or another, we were going to have an adventure. First though, before we tackled the Saach Pass, we had to get through the slightly lower-altitude Rohtang Pass (3978 m above sea level), about 50 km from Manali. There are some things in life it's best not to know until after the event, and perhaps one of them in this case was the fact that the word Rohtang translates into something like 'pile of dead bodies', in reference to the many travelers who've frozen to death while trying to make their way up and over the mountain pass.

It was raining when we woke up in Manali on the morning of day 4 – the sort of weather that, in China, would have marked the start of a difficult and probably very miserable day. This time, though, although the road ahead was going to be tough and the rain would make riding conditions potentially dangerous, at least we had really good waterproof clothing – provided by one of our sponsors, REV'IT! Not having rain suits in China had been a significant factor in some profoundly wretched days.

We were relieved to find that the road out of Manali was tarmac. But it didn't last long. After just a few kilometers, we began to ascend into thick cloud, the rain continued, and the tarmac came to an end. Soon, we were in an area of road construction, riding through thick mud and surrounded by trucks. In most other countries, a section of road like that would probably have been closed to traffic; in India, life goes on – unless you're one of the people for whom it's brought to an abrupt, needless end as a result of the total absence of the sort of bureaucratic planning and forethought that are taken for granted in most other countries. There were cars, trucks, and buses traveling in both directions along what remained of the original road, weaving a precarious path amongst all the construction traffic and the men with shovels and machinery, and apparently oblivious to, or simply unperturbed by, the huge drop down the side of the mountain.

It took us three hours to travel 50 km in mud so deep it was sometimes impossible to control the steering on the bikes. That's unnerving enough at the best of times; when one mistake might cause you to plummet hundreds of meters to your death and the front wheel of your bike persists in following its own course through the mud however tightly you hold the handlebars, it's terrifying. Ryan and I got stuck in the mud a few times and had to get off the bikes and push each other out. In the end, not only are you afraid because you know you're in very real and imminent danger of riding off the edge of the mountain, you're also physically exhausted. But, somehow, we made it to the top, where we stopped to drink Mountain Dew, eat cookies, and try to pump up our sugar levels to restore some of our vastly depleted energy.

As with every high mountain pass, the weather was totally different on the other side. The rain and thick cloud simply evaporated to give way to sunshine and clear blue skies. Suddenly, *everything* was different. We worked our way steadily down the mountain and took a left turn into a remote valley on a road that looks on the map like the scribbling of an angry child.

We did about 300 km that day and by the time we rolled into Udaipur it was dark. The hotel was horrible, but we were too exhausted to care. We had something to eat and went straight to bed. The next morning, we were on the road by 7 o'clock, heading northwest on National Highway 26, bound for Killar, which we hoped to reach by midday before tackling the Saach Pass in the afternoon and then cruising into Chamba for dinner. Of course, that wasn't what happened. Eight hours after we left Udaipur, we finally reached Killar, in the Pangi Valley – having traveled just 86 km. Sections of the road had been washed away by the torrential rain, making all the blind corners even more dangerous than they would otherwise have been, and even doing 10 kph was incredibly stressful. By the end of the day, our spirits were as bruised and battered as our bodies.

There was no mobile phone signal in the mountain villages and, for the first time since we'd set out from Delhi, we were unable to call our families that night to let them know we were okay. I guess the lack of a phone service wasn't really surprising in such a remote region; what we weren't prepared for, though, was the fact that there were no gas stations. After filling up in Manali, we hadn't seen a single gas station in the 380 km or more we'd traveled during the last couple of days. If we had enough to make it to the Saach Pass, we'd be okay – from there, it was all downhill to the next good-sized town. The problem was that the fuel gauges on our bikes weren't accurate so we didn't really know how much gas we had left. What if it wasn't enough for us to make it up the mountain to the pass?

Our priority once we hit Killar was to look for somewhere to buy fuel. While we were wandering around the village, asking people with motorbikes where they bought their gas, we met a man called Raj who was home on leave from the military, spoke good English, and offered to help us. But despite managing to buy some cans of what we guessed was black-market diesel for the support vehicle, no one was willing to sell us the petrol we needed for the bikes. It's possible there genuinely isn't any petrol for sale in those remote regions, although we got the distinct impression – from the way people shrugged their shoulders and looked uncomfortable – that we might have had more luck if Chad hadn't been holding a camera. Everyone we asked told us that they bought their petrol in the next town, although it was hard to believe that they ride their motorcycles 200 km every time they need to fill up their tanks.

By the time we realized we weren't going to find what we needed, it was too late to get back on the road. So we decided to stay in Killar that night, before heading up the mountain road to the Saach Pass the next morning. With no internet access or cell-phone coverage except a service *within* town that enabled local people to talk to each other, it looked like we weren't going to be able to make contact with our wives. Until then, we'd communicated with them regularly – almost every day – and we knew they'd be worried if they didn't hear from us that night. So we asked around and found the local 'internet guy', who had a small print and computer store, from where he sent emails and text messages for people, like a high-tech scribe, and who sent a text message to Emma to let her know, 'I'm alive. No cell coverage. Using someone else's phone. Will call you tomorrow.' Spending even 24 hours without any of the many technological aids we take for granted was strangely unnerving.

There's a lot of drinking in some of the isolated and poorer regions of India. The country's whiskey market is worth around $10 billion and more whiskey is drunk there than anywhere else in the world – the cocktail of choice seems to be whiskey and Mountain Dew. Being in a small village in a remote mountainous area, we were already very obvious outsiders, and when people start getting drunk in a situation like that, I begin to feel very much like someone they have no reason to care about. Even in cities where I feel at home, I don't like being around drunk people: they're unpredictable, and if they start getting aggressive, I don't know what they're likely to do, and that makes me uncomfortable. So that evening in Killar, when the drink began to flow and the voices grew louder, we decided it was time for an early night.

When we'd told people in Manali about the route we were planning to take, they'd said, 'No one does that route. It's really tough up there.' As we'd set out from Udaipur on the morning of day 5, I was trying not to replay those conversations in my head. We'd got up early and had a brief debate about whether or not to have breakfast at the hotel before we left. 'It's only 80 km to the next town,' one of us had said. 'We'll grab a coffee and something to eat when we get there.' Had we really come so far and learned so little? That 80 km took us eight hours and at the end of it, exhausted and hungry, Ryan wrote down the words 'the worst roads of my life'. By the end our journey, he'd probably written the same thing ten times more.

Maybe there's some formula you can use to work out if it takes you X hours to travel Y km on a flat road, it'll take you $X + Z$ hours to travel Y km on a vertical road. Of course, you'd also have to add in some factor specifically related to the fact that the road is in India. Even then, I don't think you'd end up with an equation that would solve the mathematical problem with any degree of accuracy. If I'm in London and I want to ride my motorcycle to somewhere that's 80 km outside the city, I know it's going to take me about an hour. If I want to be more precise, I can allow for variables such as the time of day and the likely volume of traffic. It still won't be much more than an hour. In India, on the other hand, if you want to know how long it will take you to get from point A to point B, you have to ask maybe fifteen or twenty people and then work out the average of all their answers.

What you also have to add into the travel-time-related equation is the fact that time doesn't mean quite the same thing in India as it does in, say, London or even Shanghai. For someone who counts the days in minutes, I find that shocking. If I can save ten minutes by doing something a certain way, I will. I've got apps on my phone to show me the fastest route to wherever I want to go. If Google provides me with two options, one of which will take me 51 minutes and the other 48, I'll follow the route that's going to save me three minutes. It's silly, I know; but it's a habit that it's hard to break. And it does have relevance in many walks of life. For example, working in the financial markets, as I did, if you aren't at your desk when the market opens, you'll miss out. It matters – in terms of what you're doing. There are people in London I could email today to arrange a meeting and they'd tell me, 'I've got a ten-minute slot in three months time,' and I'll know that if I turn up five minutes late, I'll have lost five of those ten minutes. That's one end of the spectrum. At the other end is what's called in the Caribbean 'island time'; I don't know if they have a name for it in India.

Some of the parts of the Middle Kingdom Ride that I'd enjoyed most were when we were traveling through isolated mountain regions: riding through the mountains really feels like an adventure. I'd thought a lot of India would be like that, but in fact there was little isolation after the Saach Pass – which was early in the trip – and that was a shame, because it was gorgeous. The Pir Panjal mountain range, which is in the Inner Himalayas, *is* remote by India's standards, although the fact that there's a village every 80 km or so and always traffic on the road means you're never really very far from life.

It was just after the monsoon season and the roads – which had probably never been very good – had been ravaged by the weather. Large sections had been washed away by the flooding, so for a lot of the time we were riding through thick, oily mud, which was exhausting. In places, landslides had made the road almost impassable and sometimes we had to wait for an hour or more while the rumble and debris were cleared away. On one occasion, the men working on the road tried to stop us skirting a landslide and going on up the mountain. 'Only local people can go past', they told us. 'You'll have to turn back.' That wasn't an option as far as we were concerned, and, fortunately, convincing them that we had to get through was a good deal easier and more successful than it had ever been in China.

The road up to the Saach Pass was very dangerous. In some places, even driving extremely slowly and carefully didn't make it any less scary. Sometimes, we seemed to be going straight up the side of a cliff, and sometimes the road twisted and wound around the contours of the mountain. The road surface was covered in dirt and mud, there were sheer drops on either side of us, and, occasionally, we were driving underneath huge cascading waterfalls. For Daniel, it was probably one of the toughest roads of the trip. Ryan hadn't sugar-coated it for him when he'd asked him if he wanted to come along with us on the India Ride. In fact, he'd told him it would probably be one of the hardest things he'd ever done. But nothing can really prepare you for having to drive on mountain roads like that, and Ryan and I did worry about him, and about Chad too – as well as all our gear in the car. On the plus side, there was little traffic and some amazing views – and we really did feel as though we were having an adventure.

It was on day 6 that we finally reached the Saach Pass. By that time, the effects of the high altitude were starting to kick in and we were having difficulty breathing the thin mountain air. There was a shrine at the pass – as there is at the top of every mountain in that part of the world – and our arrival coincided with the appearance of a local commuter bus, which was going in the opposite direction. It was raining, foggy, and very cold, but when the bus stopped, every one of its many passengers got out, rang the bell at the shrine, prayed, and left an offering of money. Traveling on a road like that can bring you face to face with your own mortality, especially when you're a passenger in a bus being driven by a man determined to get where he's going in the shortest possible time by cutting a ruthless swathe through other road users. So I guess a prayer and the expenditure of a few coins seem fair exchange for potentially increasing the odds of reaching your destination alive.

For Ryan and I, after we'd stopped at the shrine and gone through the pass, one of our main preoccupations was trying to avoid having to brake while following the road down the other side of the mountain. Going downhill on a motorcycle on a road as bad as that, when you hit the brakes and try to stop, not only do you have to fight the road itself; you also have to struggle to counteract the pull of gravity, which has the effect of speeding you up. But at least we were able to buy some black-market petrol for our motorcycles at the first small village we came to, which relieved us of one major worry.

The down side of the pass was as misty and cloudy as the up side had been – like some Mordoresque scene from The Lord of the Rings. But after an hour or so, as we rounded a bend in the road, the cloud disappeared, the sun came out, and spread out below our feet was the beautiful, lush greenness of the Chamba Valley. It was like riding into a completely different world. The contrast in terms of climate and terrain between one side and the other of mountains the size of the Himalayas is extraordinary. Because the rain can't cross mountains of that altitude, you climb up through an arid landscape of barren rock and gravel, and then descend into a fertile Utopia. It's a bit like getting on a plane in the snow in Toronto and getting off it again five hours later in the Caribbean, except that in the case of the Saach Pass, you go from one extreme to the other in just an hour or so.

After descending to 996 m above sea level, we rode into the town of Chamba just as it was getting dark, having had the last mountain experience of our journey.

Chapter 6
Amritsar to Rajasthan

Ryan

Although we'd been refused visas to travel to India's north-eastern border with China, we did make it to the Pakistan border, to the city of Amritsar in Punjab. We arrived in the dark on the evening of Friday, 7th September (day 7) – again breaking our rule never to ride at night. The next day was an off-bike day, for which we'd planned two main events, the first of which was a visit to the beautiful Harmandir Sahib (House of God), also known as the Golden Temple.

Sometimes, not even the best photographs can capture the indefinable quality that transforms something from beautiful to incredible. Perhaps there's something about the atmosphere of the place that can't be captured by a camera. Whatever the reason, it's true of the Golden Temple at Amritsar, which, despite the presence of thousands of visitors, had an almost tangible tranquility. Built as a Sikh temple in the sixteenth century, its upper floors were covered in gold some 200 years later – and it's spectacular. The temple itself, which is surrounded by a holy lake, has four entrances, representing the openness of the Sikh religion to people of every faith. Acceptance and equality are key aspects of Sikhism, and before you go inside the temple you have to take off your shoes, in an act that symbolizes the shedding of your status in the outside world, so that everyone enters as equals.

Colin and I aren't religious, but we *are* interested in learning about different religions and seeing them in action in the countries we visit, if only because so many of the major events that are occurring throughout the world have their roots in religious faith, as has been the case for thousands for years. The followers of almost every religion have built magnificent places of worship, and the Golden Temple certainly ranks amongst the most beautiful of them all.

Apart from its tranquil beauty, what was particularly striking about it, for me, was that there's no sense at all that money is the driving force behind the way it's run. It was a contrast that struck me even more forcibly later, when we'd visited other holy places elsewhere in India, at some of which – a prime example being the Rat Temple in Rajasthan – you got the feeling that the people in charge would have made you pay for the sour-smelling air you were breathing if only they'd been able to find a way of levying a tax on it. At the Golden Temple, however, you really did get the sense that everyone was genuinely welcome. As well as being able to bathe in the lake and stay at the temple for as long as they want to, visitors are offered a basic meal every day, free of charge.

Around 100,000 people visit the Golden Temple every day, and everyone we encountered was friendly and good-humored, which, for me, encapsulated many of the things that are amazing, positive, and heart-warming about India. By the time we left, I think we all had the same sense of inner peace and a desire to find out more about Sikhism.

After lunch, we headed off for our second main event of the day. I think I've mentioned already (several times) that India is a country of extraordinary contrasts. Anyone who wants to see both ends of the spectrum in a short space of time should do as we did: visit the Golden Temple in the morning and the ceremony that takes place daily at the Wagah border crossing in the afternoon. It was, quite literally, a case of from the sublime to the surreal.

In August 1947, British India – as it was then – was partitioned on the basis of religion into the Union (which later became the Republic) of India and the Dominion of Pakistan. The latter was subsequently divided again in 1971 into the Islamic Republic of Pakistan and the People's Republic of Bangladesh. On the partition of India, the village of Wagah (called Wahga in Pakistan) in the province of Punjab fell on the boundary between the two countries (which is known as the Radcliffe Line), so that the eastern half remained in India and the western half became incorporated into the new sovereign state of Pakistan.

It all sounds fairly straightforward when explained like that, whereas, in reality, the partition of India was mired in violence. Despite sharing many aspects of their history and culture, India and Pakistan have since been involved in numerous military conflicts, and relations between the two countries remain hostile. That hostility becomes manifest in the form of the surreal, choreographed ritual surrounding the lowering of the flags ceremony that has taken place at Wagah just before sunset every day since 1959.

On the Indian side of the border, hundreds of men and women sit – the sexes segregated – in a huge amphitheater to watch the chest-beating, foot-stomping, slick-marching, saluting, mutual show of contempt that's put on by the security forces of both sides. As the sun sets, the gates between India and Pakistan open, the flags of the two nations are lowered simultaneously, a soldier from either side steps forward, the two men shake hands, briskly and peremptorily, and then the gates slam shut again. According to something I read, 'the aggressive nature of the ceremony was toned down a couple of years ago'. It would have been interesting to see what it was like before!

Although there were spectators on both sides of the border, there were probably ten times more on the Indian side, and the noise was incredible. In true theatrical/TV-show style, someone came on first to hype-up the crowd. Then the soldiers, dressed immaculately and wearing elaborate, fan-shaped headdresses, did a sort of quick-step march across the 'stage' before performing a series of dramatically threatening hand gestures. All the time, people were dancing, the crowd was clapping and cheering, and the whole thing was great fun.

The two countries are divided by religion – Pakistan is Muslim, whereas India is basically secular – and by many other issues on which they don't see eye to eye. Despite the extraordinary and very theatrical show of belligerence, however, the ceremony clearly depended on very precisely timed and harmonious actions that resulted in the two flags being lowered in perfect unison by soldiers from the two ostensibly hostile countries.

We'd been granted permits to film the Wagah border ceremony, and Chad got some really great footage. Perhaps the most striking aspect of it all – apart from the color, noise, and strutting, almost-camp drama – was the intense national pride shown by the, mostly genial, spectators. I don't think I'd realized there was such a sense of raw nationalism in India. It was yet another interesting aspect of the country and its people.

From Amritsar, we drove south toward Bikaner, which is in the border state of Rajasthan. It was a journey that started in the cool emptiness of the Aravalli Mountain range and took us into the baking heat of the Thar Desert, where the temperature sometimes rose to 50 °C. Parts of Rajasthan form a vast wasteland between Pakistan and India, and there was little traffic on the road, other than a huge convoy of military vehicles that we seemed to be passing for almost half a day. Then, as we dropped down out of the mountains, the traffic became heavier. It was mostly trucks and massive lorries rather than local cars; but the vehicles we really had to watch out for were the buses, whose drivers seemed to have no concept of cause and effect and no fear of death.

In addition to the bus drivers, we had torrential rain to contend with – and all the potential hazards that come with it. Some 90% of the rain that falls in Rajasthan does so between July and September, when the arid, low-lying desert region is transformed into a raging torrent of flood water; we had a small taste of what that was like when we were there. As we drove across the seemingly endless, flat landscape, we could see the rainstorms coming toward us while they were still some distance away. We'd watch the sky slowly darken and then, just before the first massive raindrops began to fall, we'd stop and put on our rain suits. For the next forty minutes after we set off again, we'd barely be able to see the road in front of us.

Riding in torrential rain on any road surface in any conditions is dangerous and tiring. Riding in torrential rain on roads that are being constantly and randomly crossed by cows and, now, camels, as well as by bicycles and tuk-tuks that are vying for road space with the trucks and buses, is lethal.

The only upside to the rain was that it washed the intense heat out of the sky and brought down cooler air from above. When it stopped – which it did each time as suddenly as it had started – the sun came out again, the intense heat returned instantly, and we pulled over to the side of the road to strip off our rain suits before we were boiled alive. By the time we got back on our bikes, the water on the road was already evaporating, and rising up in front of us like clouds of steam.

It was frustrating to have to keep stopping at the approach of each rainstorm and then stopping again when it had passed over. But, in fact, we were lucky, because – as we found out later – many cities and roads in the area were very badly affected by severe flooding at the time when we were passing through the region.

When the rain stops and the countryside around you becomes visible again, you can see that parts of Rajasthan are beautiful, and it's an interesting place. The largest state in India – the name means 'land of kingdoms' – Rajasthan has a primarily Hindu population. From the sixth to the twentieth century, the vast majority of the many princely states of the region were ruled by Rajputs – members of clans who believe they are the descendants of the Hindu warriors of northern India who fought valiantly on many occasions to protect their land against Islamic and Mughal invasions. Many of Rajasthan's ancient forts and palaces are still standing today, and as well as having an impressive architectural heritage, the region has a rich culture and an economy based primarily on agriculture. In addition to growing wheat and barley, it is India's largest producer of wool and opium – and its principal consumer of the latter. It also produces crude oil and has substantial quarrying and mining industries – the white marble from which the Taj Mahal was built came from a town in Rajasthan.

In the 1980s, there was a boom in tourism in the region and many of the elaborately opulent palaces were converted into hotels. At least, that was the plan. What actually happened in a lot of cases was that conversions were started but never completed, for whatever reason. The result is that the roads are lined by partially rebuilt and badly refurbished buildings, many of them palace-themed hotels, which – despite being more like building sites than somewhere you'd want to stay for the night – actually take in paying guests. It's a beautiful but strange place.

It was during one of the torrential rainstorms that I realized I had a flat tire. The same thing had happened to me during the Middle Kingdom Ride, and on another day in China I'd blown my clutch. So one of my first thoughts on this occasion was 'Why me? Why doesn't this sort of thing happen to Colin?'

I had to shout into the microphone in my motorcycle helmet so that Colin could hear my voice above the relentless thundering of the rain. We pulled over to the side of the road, crouched down beside my bike and, with the water pounding on our backs, examined the tire.

'I think it's a slow leak,' Colin bellowed in my ear. 'If we can pump it up enough, we should be able to get to the next town without damaging the rim of the wheel. But we'll have to ride slowly.'

Twenty minutes later, Colin rode into the town of Doda and I limped in not far behind him. Because motorcycles are popular and relatively affordable in India, even small towns seem to have at least one motorcycle repair shop. And when we rolled up to the one in Doda (population approximately 25,500), the young man working there immediately stopped what he was doing, found the leak in the tire, patched it – and charged us $1! While he was doing the repair, we talked to the small crowd of grinning, chattering men and boys who'd gathered around us. We were posing for photographs with them when a man wearing flip-flops, a T-shirt, and something around his waist that looked like a cross between a towel and a sarong, stopped his motorcycle at the side of the road and pushed his way through the throng towards us. Smiling broadly, he shook my hand and said, 'I speak English. Are you okay?'

'We're fine, thanks,' I told the man. 'We're just getting our motorcycle fixed. We had a flat tire.'

'Where have you come from? And where are you going?' he asked us. We'd answered the same questions many times during the last few days, but we enjoyed the fact of people's genuine interest in what we were doing and were always ready and willing to answer them again. And the man was clearly intrigued when we explained about our trip.

'I'm on my way to Amritsar,' he told us. 'I have to get there tonight.'

'Won't that mean you'll be riding in the dark?' I asked him. 'Wouldn't it be safer to wear a helmet and some reflective gear?'

He looked at me with a bemused expression on his face. Thinking that he hadn't understood, I was about to ask the questions again when he smiled and said, as though explaining something to a rather slow-witted child, 'If I am to die on the road, that will be god's will. It will have nothing to do with wearing protective clothing.' Clearly, it was an answer that made perfect sense to him, as well as to the other men in the crowd that surrounded us, who nodded their heads in approving agreement.

As far as religion is concerned, I'm basically a supporter of the idea of 'believe whatever you like, but do no harm'. If you're going to believe in something, however, it seems to me it should be something that doesn't involve flying in the face of simple commonsense. Which is why I found the fatalism of many of the Indians we met a bit disturbing, particularly in view of the fact that some of their beliefs go a long way toward explaining the really appalling driving in the country and the very high death toll resulting from road traffic accidents.

Stopping at Doda to get the tire fixed provided us with a welcome interlude to driving in horrible road conditions exacerbated by periods of intense heat interspersed with torrential rain. But it wasn't long before we were back on the road again –

just as the clouds regrouped and the next downpour began.

We traveled 323 km that day, from Amritsar to Hanmagarth. What happened at that little repair shop in Doda was vindication of our decision to ride Royal Enfields rather than BMWs or any other make of motorcycle with expensive parts that could only have been obtained with great difficulty and fitted by mechanics with specialized skills. Three days later, the decision to choose Indian vehicles once again proved to have been a good one, although this time it was Chad and Daniel who had mechanical problems.

Colin and I always rode ahead of the support vehicle. Every now and then, when we lost sight of it in our rearview mirrors, we'd pull over to the side of the road, drink some water, and wait for Daniel to drive past before catching up with it again. All Colin and I were carrying on the motorcycles was water and enough snacks for the day. So although our top speed was only around 80 kph, the support vehicle – which was loaded with all our gear, including heavy Pelican cases containing cameras and hard drives – was even slower.

Colin and I talked to each other almost constantly while we were on the road. When the traffic was heavy, which was most of the time, our 'conversations' consisted primarily of warning each other about the crazy things all the other road users, both human and otherwise, were doing or might be about to do. It was eleven o'clock on this particular day – day 11 – and we'd been riding for about three hours when Colin said, 'Hey, I can't see the guys. When was the last time you saw them?'

I glanced in my rearview mirror as I answered, 'I don't know. In fact, I think it's been a while.'

It was a relief to stop in the shade and drink some water while we waited for them to catch up with us. But when the minutes ticked by and they still didn't appear, I phoned Chad.

'Something weird's happening,' he told me. 'We're in fifth gear, but we're only doing 30 kph.'

'How does the engine sound?' I asked – imagining for a moment that I might be able to diagnose the problem from his answer!

'It sounds ... wrong,' Chad said. 'And there's this weird smell.'

Twenty minutes later, the SUV finally came into sight and rolled in behind us at the side of the road. I don't have a huge amount of interest in what goes on under the hood of my own car, which I like to think is the only explanation for my limited mechanical skills. But even I could see as soon as we opened the hood of the SUV that there was something seriously wrong with the clutch. It was probably driving through the mountains that had caused the problem – the transmission takes a bashing when you're using the clutch all the time as you navigate steep inclines and declines.

Within seconds of the SUV pulling in at the side of the road, it seemed that at least half the local population had stopped to watch what we were doing and to discuss our predicament amongst themselves, to the accompaniment of much smiling and head waggling. Some of the bystanders helped us to push the car under the trees, so that the intense heat of the sun wouldn't melt the thousands of dollars worth of equipment it was carrying. Then I made a call to Mahindra's head office in Mumbai, where I spoke to Vinod Nookala, the guy who'd already done so much to help us.

'Please phone the Mahindra dealership in Nagaur,' he told me, after I'd explained the situation to him. 'They will be waiting for your call.'

An hour later, we were picked up by a man in a similar-looking Mahindra SUV who slung chains between the two vehicles and towed the SUV to a nearby town, where a mechanic fixed the clutch and had us back on the road within four hours.

When my BMW motorcycle developed a clutch problem during our journey around China, we'd been delayed for almost a week, and replacing it had cost us a small fortune in hotel rooms, plane tickets, and new parts for the bike. So the fact that, this time, we were on the road again within just a few hours was a huge boost to our morale.

Mahindra proved to be a really brilliant partner on the India Ride; when you're attempting a journey like the one we were doing, good support like that can prevent an inconvenience becoming a catastrophe.

Chapter 7
The Rat Temple

Colin

Ryan had read in a guidebook about the Karni Mata Temple at Deshnoke, which is approximately 30 km south of Bikaner, in Rajasthan. It was the fact of it being inhabited by more than 20,000 rats – who some people believe are their reincarnated ancestors – that made him decide it was somewhere we had to visit. The temple, which was built in the early 1900s, is named after a fourteenth-century Hindi mystic who was believed to be the incarnation of the goddess Durga. According to the story, as members of Karni Mata's clan died, they were reborn as rats to await reincarnation. For obvious reasons, it's also known as the Rat Temple.

To many people, a building full of rats might sound like something conjured up in a fever-induced nightmare. I'd like to be able to say they'd be wrong, but I can't. I don't have any fear of rodents, but this was something else. Although I'm not a religious person – I don't believe in any god – I do accept that, for whatever reason, some people need to put their faith in something spiritual. So even if I don't understand what someone has chosen to believe, I have to respect it – even if it's rodent ancestors – while I'm in their place of worship. What was really hard to accept, however, was how badly managed and poorly maintained the temple was, and the fact that the people running it were apparently preying on other people's religious convictions for their own financial gain.

We had an Indian fixer in Delhi who'd organized a permit to allow us to film inside the temple. When we actually got there and they saw our camera and realized that *we* weren't Indian, we were told it was going to cost considerably more than the amount that had been agreed. The problem was that although refusing to pay might have felt morally satisfying, it would also have meant not being able to film at all. 'No cash payment, no filming': you're screwed and they know it. And as one of the two major purposes of our journey around India was to make a documentary, it would simply have been like shooting ourselves in the foot.

We'd gone to the temple wanting to tell the story of how people travel from all over the country, and beyond, to visit the rats they believe to be their ancestors, and we felt as though we'd been scammed by a bunch of gangsters. Much the same thing happened almost everywhere we went in India. It's annoying and it puts you off doing any dealings at all with the people involved; but it's the way things are, and, ultimately, there's no point arguing about it.

Charging a higher price to foreigners who clearly have money at their disposable is reasonable enough if you use that money advisedly. I don't think any of us would have minded quite so much about the sticky fingers of the guys managing the Rat Temple if it hadn't been for the state of the place and for the fact that, rather than the extra money going toward its upkeep, it was clearly going to go straight into their pockets. The conditions in the temple were horrific, and walking around it raised all sorts of questions in my mind.

I suppose any really strongly held belief exposes the believer to exploitation. Taking advantage of all the people who genuinely believe that the rats are their ancestors and failing to keep the place clean seems to me to be very little different from taking advantage of children. If I thought my ancestors were amongst those rats, I'd want them to have a nice place to live and I'd want to know that any money I was donating to the temple was going to be spent to that end. It's like visiting the grave of someone you've loved and finding the cemetery full of weeds and dog crap. You'd be very upset and you'd want to know what the hell was going on. What was really sad, though, was the fact that the visitors to the Rat Temple seemed simply to accept the appallingly disgusting state of the place and handed over their entry fee willingly and without complaint.

Maybe the really strong feeling of distaste we all had about the

Rat Temple was partly a factor of expectation: what's acceptable in terms of levels of cleanliness in one place isn't acceptable in another, and you expect a temple to be clean. Or maybe it had more to do with religion and with the realization that it really does dominate the daily lives of people in India, perhaps more than it does in many other countries. For someone like me, who's always asking questions, the thought of waking up every morning 'knowing' that every decision that might need to be made has already been made for you – which is 'knowledge' that's actually based on blind faith – is mind-boggling.

A lot of religions are underlined by sound principles that people *should* live by. But then a load of other fringe beliefs gets piled on top of those principles until you can no longer see the wood for the trees. It's the creation and dissemination of all those additional beliefs that result in some guy riding a motorcycle without a helmet or any form of protective clothing because he 'knows' that whether or not he arrives at his destination has nothing to do with anything he might do but is all in the lap of the gods. That's ridiculous! I simply don't understand how, in this day and age, when people have access to an almost infinite amount of information on the internet, they still believe things that are so patently unbelievable.

In the days when I had my own company in Toronto – which seems a very long time ago but actually isn't – there was a guy who worked for me who, as a recovering party-drug-addict, became a born-again Christian. It really helped him to put his life back on track: he got married, had a couple of kids, started making money, and was happy. You have to accept that something which helps someone put the brakes on a life that's careering toward self-destruction and then turn it around can't be bad. If religious belief is what provides you with the structure you need to enable you to stop sitting in bars every day, drinking, taking drugs, and watching your life disappear down the tubes, then that's fine. In a case like that, religion acts as a life raft; although, in reality, there are things other than religion that could well have had the same effect.

Being in India made me realize more than anything else has ever done that the evolution of humankind has to be based on education. In certain sectors of the country, the education system is good; in others, the vast majority of people don't have access to schooling and therefore they are likely to grow up to become adults with a very narrow, child-like focus on the world. If you haven't had access to education, you can't read; if you can't read, your only source of information is other people, and you have no way of assessing the veracity of what they tell you. What we experienced in India made me understand how important it is that people learn to read, so that they can ask questions, find answers to those questions themselves, and don't end up going to a filthy, dilapidated Rat Temple to visit their ancestors. (If I die tomorrow and turn up as a rat in Deshnoke, I'm going to feel like a fool.)

For the rats, on the other hand, living in the Karni Mata Temple must be close to obtaining Nirvana – in some respects, at least. Able to run free and procreate at will, they have no natural enemies within the confines of the temple itself and the surrounding courtyard. As they scuttle and scurry in heaving masses across the marble floors, over ledges and door handles, and along every other conceivable surface, they are protected by means of grilles and wire netting from potential predators such as birds and snakes. And they're provided with an almost infinite supply of food, which is bought by visitors to the temple.

Every dish of milk and fragment of coconut shell is almost completely swamped by fat, grey-furred, docile but unhealthy-looking rats. There are thousands of them, and there are thousands more with matted coats and skin covered in sores and scabs, that are clearly diseased and in various stages of dying. Apparently, caretakers are employed to sweep up all the rat excrement – I can't even imagine how much urine and feces is produced by more than 20,000 overfed rats in a 24-hour period – and to dispose of the thousands of dead and decaying bodies.

The math is fairly basic: if there are, say, 25,000 rats living in conditions of adequate food supply, X percent will give birth every day and Y percent will die of old age or other natural causes. It's the whole circle-of-life thing. What it doesn't take into account, though, are the deaths from diabetes and all the other diseases that are rife as a result of all the sugary foods that are fed to the rats. In natural conditions, factors such as the amount of food available exert some control over population numbers. When there's an almost infinite supply of (mostly inappropriate) food and no predators, there's going to be overcrowding and, unless heroic efforts are made to maintain a very high level of hygiene and cleanliness, that will result in ill-health and the rapid spread of disease. So perhaps the caretakers do try to keep pace with cleaning out all the dead animals but are fighting an almost impossible battle. We didn't see any real sign of their endeavors, however, and the whole place was indescribably filthy. It certainly wasn't anything like the rat sanctuary we'd expected it to be; it was more like a horrible, skin-crawling, disease-infested nightmare.

While we were there, looking at the temple and trying not to do or say anything that would be disrespectful to all the visitors who believed that the rats were their ancestors, we were all wondering the same thing: were we going to catch some horrible disease? You couldn't avoid standing in the excrement of what was clearly a very large number of sick animals: it covered the entire floor. Lots of people were petting the rats and feeding them with their hands, and whereas I was afraid of touching *anything*, Ryan actually stroked one! Eating food that has been 'tasted' by a rat is considered to be 'a good thing', and quite a few of the visitors were eating sweets or drinking milk after rats had nibbled at them. So maybe there *is* something special about the Karni Mata Temple – there has to be some reason why the people who visit it don't all become seriously ill. Perhaps they've already built up resistance, or maybe some of them *do* get ill afterwards but no one realizes that the two events are connected.

Apart from eating food that's already been chewed on by a rat, another thing that's supposed to be a blessing is having a rat scuttle across your feet. It was something I'd have done almost anything to avoid. Although most of the Indian visitors to the temple were barefoot, we were allowed to keep our socks on. By the time we left, they were covered in rat piss and feces. It was difficult not to retch as we peeled them off our stinking feet and threw them in the garbage.

Best of all the blessings is seeing a white rat. Apparently, there are only about ten white rats living in the temple, which are thought to be the reincarnations of Karni Mata herself and of her four sons. (We didn't manage to discover who the other six used to be.) When we spotted one, we were almost as delighted as the other visitors who'd been searching with us.

Whereas it was Daniel's first experience of traveling in a country with a culture that is, in many respects, very unlike the one he's used to, Chad, Ryan, and I have been to some remote locations, slept in damp and dirty places, eaten strange, sometimes horrible food, and consider ourselves to be quite hardy adventurers. But this was something completely different. Chad was filming, so he was walking around focused on that and being very professional, while Ryan and I were struggling to suppress our instinctive, almost emotional responses to what we were seeing and make some sort of sense of it.

Above all, we wanted to be culturally sensitive, not least because most of the other people there actually believed they were in the presence of their ancestors. So we didn't want to walk around looking shocked or disdainful and saying, 'Ooh, that's nasty!' But there were occasions when it was difficult to hide our disgust at the squalor and at the appalling, filthy conditions the rats were living in – and through which all those people were walking in their bare feet. We were very aware of being tourists in a place that was sacred to most of the other people there, and during the two hours we spent in the temple, talking to camera and trying to convey our feelings about what we were seeing without insulting anyone, we sometimes had to focus very hard to stop ourselves throwing up.

I'd like to be able to say that something good came out of our experience that day. The truth is, however, that it was both stomach-churning and disappointing. It was depressing, too, to see how a small number of people were taking advantage and making money out of the genuine beliefs of others. As we left, Ryan and I tried – but failed – to think of anywhere we'd ever seen that was dirtier, less sanitary, and less uplifting than the Karni Mata Temple.

Chapter 8
They make wine in India

Colin

From Bikaner, we traveled south through flat terrain and incredible heat to Nagaur and then down to Udaipur, where we stayed for three days. On the last day, I got sick. I think it was food poisoning. Whatever caused it, there were moments during the ten hours it took us to ride 380 km to Vadodara, in Gujarat, when I almost wished I could lie down at the side of the road and die. I'd woken up at about 4 o'clock that morning feeling horrible, and it turned out to be one of the worst days of my life. I didn't actually vomit, but it was as though I was fighting something off. I felt like you do when you have flu and every part of your body aches so much that it just hurts to be alive.

There was no point staying another day in Udaipur: I'd feel just as ill lying in bed in a hotel as I would on the road. Or so I thought. In reality, being on the bike intensified the already severe throbbing pain in all my muscles. That day made all the tough days that followed seem less tough by comparison, and at least, while I was riding, I was forced to focus on something other than how bad I was feeling. I was light-headed and chilled; despite wearing a long-sleeved shirt in an air temperature of around 35 °C, my whole body was constantly bathed in cold sweat. Sometimes, I felt so weak and disorientated I could barely hold myself upright on the bike and I'd suddenly realize I was almost lying on the fuel tank. The only slight reprieve I had was when we stopped every hour or so and I sank down onto the dirt at the side of the road, where I lay with my back flat on the ground and my legs raised.

That night, after an achingly miserable day, we stayed in a hotel in Vadodara, where I ate a bit of food, rehydrated as much as I could, and passed out for the next fourteen hours. Looking back on it now, it was stupid to have pushed on that day, when I wasn't able to focus 100% on the road. What we should have done was stop until I'd recovered, or at least until I felt a bit better. I don't know why we didn't do that. It was my fault though: I was the one who insisted on going on. I suppose part of the reason was because we all felt under pressure to keep to the schedule. It was a day I was lucky to survive. Once again, it was the bus drivers, particularly, who made riding a motorcycle without full concentration so incredibly dangerous. I'd begun to wonder if they'd all seen Speed, and if that's why they drive down the middle of the road, horns blaring, and don't stop, or even slow down, for anything or anyone.

When I woke up the next morning, I didn't feel a great deal

better. My body was completely shattered, but at least I knew I wasn't going to die after all – not from food poisoning anyway – which was good, because I was looking forward to our next stop, at the Sula Vineyards at Nashik, about 1000 m above sea level in the hills some 180 km north-east of Mumbai.

Before starting to plan the India Ride, Ryan and I had had no idea that the country produced any wine, or even that there were parts of it where the climate is conducive to growing grapes suitable for viniculture. Although a lot of alcohol is drunk in India, it's mostly cheap whiskey and beer – impoverished people don't drink fine wines. But, due to the rising incomes of recent years, which have resulted in a burgeoning middle class, there's been an increase in wine consumption. Ryan had come across the Sula Vineyards by chance, on the internet, and he'd arranged for us to stay at the resort in the mountains and have a guided tour.

The top speed of our motorcycles was 80-85 kph. Throughout almost all our journey around India, that was enough to make us the fastest vehicles on the road, which meant that we only had to worry about what was going on ahead of us. As we approached Nashik, however, and later as we got close to Mumbai, we started being passed by BMWs and Audis, and as the cars got better, the traffic moved faster and we had to make a real adjustment to the way we'd been driving. Suddenly we were in a wealthier part of India and we couldn't rely on just looking ahead all the time: we had to keep checking behind too, to see what was about to overtake us or pull in beside us in an attempt to avoid being hit by an oncoming vehicle, pushing us into the path of another car in the process.

If you go from London, for example, to some posh resort in the countryside, the landscape might change a bit, but the contrast isn't very remarkable; whereas the difference between Mumbai and Sula Vineyards is stark. It's like entering a completely different world. After a really tough day's riding, as we started to get closer to Nashik, the countryside became undulating and the air grew gradually cooler and fresher.

I spend quite a lot of money on good wine, although I'm by no means a connoisseur. I think I might be too lazy to become an expert on anything. There's a finite amount of space in my brain for storing information and when it comes to wine, I choose to respect the decisions made by other people who know what they're talking about. I was looking forward to this bit of the trip, however; partly because vineyards mean countryside and I really enjoy spending time in the country, just relaxing. All of which made it even more disappointing that I still felt so ill.

When we arrived at the hotel at Nashik, at around 5 p.m. on day 16, I had a shower, ate some bread, collapsed into bed, and slept until 7 o'clock the next morning. I still didn't feel good when I woke up, but we'd come a long way to visit the vineyards, and I knew that it was my duty to suppress any lingering

---

[2] A movie (1994) in which a disaffected retired bomb squad sergeant puts a bomb on a city bus that will detonate if its speed drops below 50 mph.

sickness, step up, be a man, and taste the wine!

The vineyards themselves create a peaceful oasis that's the complete antithesis of the super-hot, overcrowded chaos of India's cities and of the roads we'd left behind us earlier that day. In fact, everything about the winery and associated hotel – including the hospitality, facilities, and sheer beauty of the place – made it seem as though we'd stepped out of India and into an expensive resort in Tuscany or rural France. Being there was one of several occasions during the journey when I felt as though I'd time warped away from India. We'd ridden through impoverished countryside into a world frequented by Bollywood stars, business executives, and other middle-class, wealthy people who live and work in Mumbai and who want somewhere to go at the weekends to get away from the heat, noise, and crazy pace of life in the city.

In a country with a population of more than 1.2 billion, if just 1% are millionaires, that's 12 million very rich people – more than one-third of the entire population of Canada – who are looking for places to go to spend their money. And Sula Vineyards is one of those places, as well as being another example of what people in India can do if they're given the chance. The only question in my mind is: if I were a resident of Mumbai, would I think it was worth all the effort involved to drive up into the hills to Nashik? In China, having seen the potential of an area where grapes have been grown for many years, a good road would probably be built before the resort itself was developed. That doesn't seem to be the way things are done in India.

We stayed in Nashik for less than 24 hours. When we arrived in the evening, we had a really beautiful dinner, did some wine tasting, and sat outside in air that was so cool we needed sweaters. It was the first time in more than two weeks that we didn't feel as though we were melting. The next morning, after breakfast, we took a tour of the vineyards and winery.

As well as using their own grapes, Sula Vineyards makes a whole range of wines from grapes grown by local farmers – including shiraz, merlot, sauvignon blanc, and sparkling wines – which are already popular in India and are becoming increasingly recognized and available internationally. The founder and CEO of the company was born and raised in Mumbai, went to university in the USA and then worked in Silicon Valley in California, before returning to India and establishing the winery in 1999. During its first year of production, Sula Vineyards sold 50,000 bottles; a decade later, that figure had reached 3 million. There are now 35 wineries in Nashik, which has become the wine capital of India. As far as possible, the grapes are grown and the wine is produced on the basis of sustainable and environmentally friendly principles, and the vineyards and winery provide employment for a substantial number of local people.

The resort is set in gorgeous countryside amidst lush rolling hills that stretch as far as the eye can see and as well as great restaurants, it has a hotel with a swimming pool and spa. It would have been nice to have been able to stay there longer – maybe even a week – but you soften up if you take a break of more than a couple of days, and then, when you get back on the bike, you go through all the business of aching muscles again.

We left Nashik at noon the next day and headed down the mountain toward Mumbai. Once again, we had to concentrate on dodging all the vehicles being driven by drivers who see a gap in the central barrier and suddenly veer blindly across the road in front of you. For motorcycles, particularly, the tuk-tuks are like landmines: that afternoon alone, Daniel came close to hitting one in the SUV and Ryan missed two by breathtakingly narrow margins. By mid-afternoon, the heat was intense and we were very tired. And then, at the bottom of a very steep hill, we saw the aftermath of a terrible accident. It looked as though the brakes on a truck had failed and as it tried to pull into the side of the road, it had flipped over onto a tuk-tuk.

By the time we arrived on the scene, there was a crowd of people standing around a woman who was sitting in the dust, wailing as she cradled a crushed, blood-soaked body in her arms. It looked as though there were two other bodies under the truck. It was an incredibly shocking sight. Believing in fate clearly doesn't in any way lessen the extreme pain you feel when you're holding the dead body of someone you love.

It wasn't the first time I'd seen someone die. That was in the winter in Toronto, when a friend and I were driving along a road and saw an elderly man lose his footing on the icy pavement and fall. I stopped the car and we called 911 and tried to help him. But he'd hit his head on the ground and he died right there in our arms while we were waiting for the ambulance to arrive. It was a tragic accident and deeply upsetting. Somehow though, the fact that it was just shitty luck seemed to make it less disturbing in retrospect than the accident we came across that day on the east coast highway in India, which was almost certainly avoidable.

Seeing those dead bodies at the side of the road reminded us just how fragile our own lives are and how dangerous it is to drive on any road in India. And it made me angry, too. On the one hand, you see the terrible sadness death brings and, on the other, you come face to face with people's apparently total lack of awareness that doing something extremely dangerous – like swerving a rickshaw across the road in the direct path of fast-moving traffic – is going to get you killed.

What might also have been a contributing factor to that accident on the road to Mumbai – and to at least a proportion of the many other road accidents that occur in India every day – is the fact that most of the vehicles are poorly maintained. The problem is that maintenance costs money, so when something breaks, it doesn't get fixed, which means that, in the countryside particularly, you often see trucks and cars that appear to be held together with duck tape.

Back in the searing heat and anarchic disorder of the city,

They make wine in India

we checked into the Westin Hotel in Mumbai, where our rooms, on floor thirty-something, had spectacular views that seemed almost surreal after the tranquil beauty of Mumbai. We'd been on the road for seventeen days; we'd completed one-third of the India Ride, and we thought we'd already experienced pretty much everything India could throw at us.

We spent the next two nights in Mumbai, swimming in the hotel pool, eating, sleeping, and taking a real break. During that time, we only filmed once, outside on the streets, where Ryan was almost attacked by a dog that took an unprovoked dislike to him and jumped out at him, barking ferociously. It was the evening and we stood for a while on an overpass, watching all the buses on the roads below us and the dense swirling mass of commuters making their way home. There seemed to be a lot of men just standing around, and as soon as we started filming we attracted a large, inquisitive crowd. Mumbai has a rich history, but its sites are already very well known, and filming them wasn't really what our journey was all about. So we didn't explore the city in any depth – with a population of 20 million, it could have taken us three hours or more just to cross town.

As we were leaving Mumbai on the morning of day 19, Ryan had a fall. Fortunately, it wasn't a bad one. We were on a side road, doing about 20 kph, so apart from bruising his ribs, he didn't come to any real harm, although the fact that the event was caught on four cameras might have put a small dent in his pride!

Chapter 9
Pune

Ryan ─────────────────────────

We'd followed a route southwest from Nashik to Mumbai through a wealthy part of India that continued as we drove southeast for about another 150 km into the mountains to Pune, where we'd booked into a good hotel. And it was as we arrived in Pune that we had the only negative experience of our stay there.

In China, motorcycles aren't welcome at good hotels. It's a countrywide attitude based on the concept that people only ride motorcycles because they can't afford to drive a car. So even if you turn up on a very costly BMW motorcycle – as we did during the Middle Kingdom Ride – you're met with hostility and hustled away to unpack your bike out of sight of the hotel entrance. It had been a recurring theme in China, which led to some angry confrontations. But I hadn't expected to have the same experience in India, particularly in view of the fact that India has a substantial motorcycle community and motorcycling as a leisure activity is very popular amongst the many people who *choose* to buy motorcycles. So I was taken by surprise when we pulled up at the main entrance of the hotel in Pune, started to unpack the bikes and the SUV, and were accosted by an irate hotel employee, telling us urgently, 'No two wheels allowed at hotel entrance.'

'We are guests at the hotel,' I told the guy, through gritted teeth. I was hot and tired; I had fallen off my motorcycle just a few hours earlier and my ribs were bruised and battered. The last thing I wanted was to get involved in any kind of argument.

'You park there,' he said, waving his hand peremptorily in the direction of the car park.

'We *will* park there.' I paused, took a deep breath, and then said, very slowly, 'But first we're going to unpack all our gear, carry it into the hotel, take off our jackets, find our passports, and check in. When we've done all that, we'll park our bikes, just like we'd do if we'd arrived in a car.'

When you've been riding all day – on any roads, let alone on hot, chaotic, death-trap roads – the image you have in your head of the hotel you're going to be staying in is almost like an oasis in the desert. When the going gets really rough, you focus on that hotel: you imagine standing under the shower, washing away all the sweat and dirt that's accumulated on every inch of your body; you run through in your mind the phone conversation you're going to have with your wife; you visualize yourself sitting under a large ceiling fan in a cool, airy dining room, wearing clean clothes, drinking a beer, and eating a great meal, before lying down on a comfortable bed, resting your head on a soft pillow, covering yourself with a white, newly laundered sheet, and falling asleep.

So when you finally arrive at the hotel, knowing that all the things you've been imagining for the last few exhausting hours are now just a few steps away, on the other side of a set of glass doors, and then you look up to find a security guard standing in front of you like some belligerent St Peter at the gates of heaven, you tend to lose your cool. Every time it's happened, it's almost as if some switch flicks on inside my head, making me absolutely determined that I'm going to do this thing *my* way.

Where discrimination against motorcycles and motorcyclists exists, it tends to be non-specific: I'm sure if Tom Cruise rode up to one of these hotels riding the most expensive motorcycle money can buy, he'd be told exactly the same thing as we were told – 'No two wheels allowed at hotel entrance.' What I actually heard every time it was said to us was, 'If you're on a two-wheeler, you're a second-class citizen. So park your bike over there!'

Colin and I would arrive at the hotels very tired and dirty, and the last thing we wanted on those occasions was to get embroiled in some ridiculous, frustratingly pointless argument. The more often it happened, the more it mattered to me, and the more I wanted to shout at the guy, 'Get out of my way and let me check in.' In China, we'd leave those hotels the next morning having paid a bill of several hundred dollars, which was an amount of money that I felt entitled me, if nothing else did, to unload my motorcycle at the front door.

But that was China, and now we were in India, where I hadn't expected to encounter the same prejudice. It happened to us for the first time in Pune, and then many other times after that. In fact, at one hotel the guy started screaming at us, until the manager came running out, apologizing profusely. On another occasion, later in the trip, a security guard attempted to stop us and when Colin and I just blew past him, he chased after us and tried to jump on one of the bikes. That was the final straw as far as I was concerned. After that, whenever we were booked into decent hotels, I'd call ahead and tell them, 'These are our license-plate numbers; this is the type of motorcycle we're riding. We're going to drive our bikes to the hotel entrance, unpack, and then park them wherever you want us to park them. We don't want anyone to try to stop us and we don't want any problems.' And, to our vast relief, it worked.

In the greater scheme of things, it probably sounds like a lot of trivial, high-handed fuss about nothing. At the time though, it was a really big deal for me. By the end of every day, I was always exhausted by the stress of having spent several incredibly hot hours trying to stay alive – and doing what I could to make sure Colin did too – while sharing the roads with hundreds of insane drivers apparently hell-bent on rigorously testing the concept of fate. At the end of a day like that, your nerves are already strung as tight as violin strings, and it doesn't take much to make them snap.

The reason we'd taken a slight detour inland from Mumbai to Pune was to visit an automobile factory. An urban agglomeration with a mostly Hindu population of about 5 million, Pune is an ancient city of cultural and educational significance that has moved with the times to become a modern center for information technology. The town also has a burgeoning automobile manufacturing industry: General Motors, Volkswagen, and Fiat all have facilities there, as does one of our sponsors on the India Ride, the Indian company Mahindra.

As a photo-journalist, I've done a lot of stories about cars in China, so I was keen to look at car manufacture in India while we were there. One aspect I'm particularly interested in is the role of car purchases as an indicator of a burgeoning economy and an expanding middle class. During the last few years, car sales have gone through the roof in China: most people there don't get married until they've got an apartment and a car, which I suppose are the two most visible signs of independence and, perhaps, of having a place in society. In India, too, as the middle class expands, more people have more money and therefore more disposable income, so consumerism has begun to build.

There are some other interesting and wide-ranging effects of a growing economy too. For example, the massive growth in car ownership in China has already changed many aspects of the dynamics of life there, because when more people own cars, more roads have to be built, which means that the infrastructure of the country improves and previously remote areas become accessible. I wanted to see if the same thing was happening in India, and visiting a car-manufacturing plant seemed like a good way to find out. So we'd scheduled an off-bike day in Pune, almost all of which we ended up spending in the Mahindra factory there.

Having spent virtually every waking hour since we'd arrived in Delhi more than three weeks earlier trying not to become engulfed by the swirling chaos all around us, everything about the massive, incredibly high-tech, well-organized, clean, state-of-the-art factory we visited was mind blowing. You could spend days in India and then leave the country again believing that nothing there is run efficiently or with any semblance of order. In some respects, the apparently anarchic, clamoring, laissez-faire way everything seems to be done is part of the country's charm. It's a charm that ceases to beguile, however, when you almost get wiped out on the road for the simple reason that, if there *are* any rules, no one knows or cares what they are. Then, just when you think you're beginning to have some understanding of how it all works, you go somewhere like the car factory in Pune and see a whole different side of the people and of the country's potential. India is a land of extraordinary contrasts. During the day we spent in Pune, we witnessed once again what *can* be done when people's energy and skills are organized and focused.

What was also interesting for me was seeing the very different way things are done in India compared to China. Government and industry in China are inextricably linked, which, although sometimes clearly a bad thing, means that the government is driving forward manufacturing in the country. That doesn't seem to happen in India, where the government apparently lags a long way behind what private industry is capable of doing. At the Mahindra factory, however, it was clear that, with or without government support, private industry was getting on with it, doing its own thing, and doing it very successfully.

The company manufactures SUVs, small cars, and massive eighteen-wheeler trucks that are primarily intended for the rapidly expanding domestic market, although some of them are exported to Europe and Africa. Colin acted as a guinea-pig for some dexterity training before doing a test that involved putting a bolt in position and screwing it down within forty-five seconds. After that, we were given a tour of the whole facility, which included having access to all areas and being able to talk to the workers – all of whom, except in the offices, were men, who spoke to us openly and with what appeared to be genuine friendliness. Living in China, I'm used to visiting somewhere like that and being told, 'No, you can't go into that room. You can't see this thing or that thing.' So it was nice to be allowed – even encouraged – to open any door we wanted to open and see whatever we wanted to see.

Every hour, the workers get a tea break. A bell rings and they run across the factory floor to some seats, where they sit and drink their tea, until it rings again ten minutes later, when they all run back to their places on the production line. For the rest of every hour, the atmosphere throughout the factory is one of industrious calm. The machinery is incredible: some of the machines can weld in a hundred different places in one minute, and then do the whole thing all over again. It's the kind of stuff I love photographing. Chad and Daniel clearly loved it too and they got some great film footage.

That day in Pune, we quite literally stepped through a door into somewhere that was, in almost every way, the antithesis of almost everything we'd experienced so far in India. Outside the factory was the hot, over-crowded, hectic disorder of the streets, astonishing poverty, and people living their lives based on an extraordinarily fatalistic philosophy that seems to tether them to the past and prevent them from helping themselves. Inside, the temperature was cool, there was an atmosphere of calm, well-organized, and efficient industry, as well as high-tech machinery that could probably match any that's used anywhere else in the world.

Walking through the door of the factory that day was like being shown what people in India can do when they're given the chance. I had a heartening sense that we were seeing the country's future, and that, contrary to what I might previously have believed, it's moving inexorably forward. Maybe it isn't progressing along a path as smooth and well-ordered as the one created by the production line in Mahindra's state-of-the-art factory; but it's definitely moving forward.

Before we visited the vineyards at Sula, we'd begun to wonder if India was in the sort of trouble it wasn't going to be able to pull itself out of. After we'd been to Sula, Mumbai, and then the car factory in Pune, we felt differently. Perhaps the country will have a bright future after all. It certainly has a lot of motivated, highly intelligent, and able people who, if given the opportunity, could replicate elsewhere the efficiency and good practice we witnessed that day.

All the outsourcing that's done in India – in call centers for banks etc. – provides jobs for local people. Ultimately, however, it's industry that creates value. What we saw in Pune made me realize that people in India are willing and able to make the sort of high-quality products that modern consumers demand, and they have the potential to do great things for themselves.

It can be wearing waking up every morning and getting on the bikes knowing that, whatever happens, you're going to have to push on. So it was nice to do something that day that took us off the road and into another mindset, and we left the factory feeling upbeat.

In fact, the day we spent in Pune was my thirty-fourth birthday, and it wasn't a coincidence that I'd arranged an off-bike day. Exactly two years earlier, we'd been just over a month into the Middle Kingdom Ride when the clutch on my motorcycle had blown out. In many places in many countries, having to replace the clutch on a BMW bike wouldn't be a big deal. In China, however, it had proved to be a frustrating and expensive breakdown that had set us back several days. I'm not exactly superstitious, but I'd decided that, given a choice, I would do what I could to reduce the risk of anything similar happening this time. I'd already fallen on the way out of Mumbai and although I hadn't been seriously hurt, my body was still aching. So it was a relief to have spent the day doing something enjoyable and to have got through it without anything bad happening.

If I'd been paying attention that night, I might have heard the sound of the gods laughing.

Chapter 10
The wonderful Mr Azad

Colin

The many manufacturing plants around Pune have made it quite a wealthy, cosmopolitan town. It's interesting to see what happens when a country starts to move away from purely independent trading and people get well-paid, secure jobs with corporations. Once someone starts working for an international company and can rely on regular paychecks, they can borrow money from a lender who knows they'll be able to pay it back, and that means they can buy a car and take out a mortgage on their own home. So they start to lead a middle-class lifestyle and to have disposable income, which in turn has a knock-on effect on other people.

After the off-bike day in Pune – which was planned by Ryan to avoid riding on his birthday – we left there the next day and were on a good but undulating road through the hills when I heard Ryan's voice in the speaker in my helmet saying, 'You're not going to believe this, but something's wrong. My bike's starting to lose power.'

'Stop at the side of the road,' I told him, 'and I'll have a look.'

Unlike many of the people who go on motorcycle adventures – and unlike many of the people who followed us online, on Facebook and Twitter – Ryan and I have little competence when it comes to repairing motorcycles. We don't know what's wrong with them when they break down and we don't know how to fix them. Riding a motorcycle adds another dimension to any journey and allows you to become part of the environment you're traveling through. But, for us, the bikes are simply the tools of the adventure and not the adventure itself. I'm a bit more hands-on than Ryan, however. So I rode his bike around a bit to test it out, although you didn't need to be a qualified mechanic to work out that the hot smell and the steam coming off the engine were indications that something was badly wrong.

We were only about 5 km out of Pune, so we had two options: we could go back to the city, where we knew we'd find someone who would be able to fix it; or we could limp on and risk the bike breaking down completely. It was only 9 a.m., which meant that if we did go back to Pune, we could probably get the bike fixed and be on our way again in time to get where we needed to be before dark. That's what we'd just decided to do when a guy on a motorcycle pulled up beside us and asked, 'Is something wrong with your bike?'

'Yes,' we told him. 'We need to find a repairman.'

He looked at us for a moment and then did that rather

disconcerting lateral head-wobbling that indicates assent, before kicking his bike back into life and saying, 'Okay. Follow me.'

Ignoring the steam and the acrid smell of something overheating, Ryan started up his motorcycle and rode cautiously down the hill after our new friend, followed by me and then Chad and Daniel in the SUV. The first place we stopped was a shack at the side of the road where a guy with some basic tools, oil, and chain lube said he couldn't fix Enfields himself but that there was another guy about a kilometer further down the road who could. We got back on our bikes and again followed the man who'd stopped to help us, until we reached another shack on the outskirts of Pune that had a sign outside it saying Azad Motors. We'd certainly never have found it on our own, not least because it looked more like a junk shop than a motorcycle repair shop. We turned to thank our Good Samaritan, but he'd disappeared, presumably having already resumed his journey to wherever it was he'd been going when he stopped to help us. We didn't even know his name.

Our next bit of good fortune that day came in the form of Mr Azad himself, the proprietor of the ramshackle tin shed at the side of the road and a constantly smiling, helpful, skilled, super-nice guy who specializes in fixing Royal Enfields. Although Mr Azad doesn't speak much English, the two young college students whose bike he was fixing when we arrived spoke it perfectly, and they translated for us. Word must have spread quickly about the foreigners in town, and it wasn't long before a friendly, inquisitive crowd of people had gathered to watch and comment on everything that was taking place.

That day in Mr Azad's motorcycle repair shop was an interesting illustration of how different people in India are from people in China and how they don't share the wariness of most Chinese about getting involved in other people's business. In societies in which thinking outside the box isn't something that's rewarded, people want to stay under the radar and not draw attention to themselves, which means that they're afraid to say or do anything different or original for fear of how it might be interpreted. That doesn't happen in India: when people saw some foreigners doing something that looked interesting, most of them didn't put their heads down and pretend not to have noticed, as people did in China; they came over and talked to us, wanting to know who we were and what we were doing. I guess the fact that so many people in India speak English is relevant too.

It turned out that Ryan's motorcycle had run out of oil – which accounted for the smell of hot metal grinding on hot metal. You need an oil change after the first 1000 km on a new bike – or 10,000 km with some of the synthetic oils; after which, it should be good for several thousand kilometers more. Before we arrived in Delhi to pick up our bikes, the guy we bought them from put around 500 km on them and then did an oil change. Ryan's bike wasn't leaking, so for it to be fresh out of oil – while my bike was fine – didn't make any sense. Ryan's explanation was that it was either eating oil for some reason or it hadn't been filled up properly when the first oil change was done. Maybe! I have no idea what my brother does to his motorcycles.

The morning we spent at Mr Azad's repair shop was one of those re-energizing experiences that can turn something bad into something good. Helped by his young son and by his brother, Mr Azad put aside everything else he'd been doing and concentrated on getting us back on the road as quickly as possible. When someone stepped out in front of Ryan as we were leaving Mumbai and he'd had to brake so suddenly that he crashed and fell, his front wheel got bent and bits of his bike were broken. So Mr Azad straightened his wheel, welded all the broken bits, and tuned up both the bikes as well as changing their oil – all of which cost us just $50 and provided us with some good film footage.

What also came out of that experience with the wonderful Mr Azad was further confirmation of the fact that we'd been right to choose to ride Royal Enfields in India. That day was saved by a local repairman working in a shack at the side of the road because he had the spare parts and the skills required to enable us to resume our journey with minimal delay. It's something that wouldn't have been possible if we'd been riding super-computerized foreign bikes assembled from complex and expensively machined parts.

Another aspect that was highlighted that day was how hard it sometimes is to stay on schedule and how doing so often wouldn't be possible at all if it weren't for the people like Mr Azad who put aside their own concerns and helped us when they had no real need to do so. When you're planning a motorcycle trip linked to a television production, the schedule is king. If it starts to slip, a minor rock fall can quickly become a landslide: you might be two or three days behind, and then, before you know it, that's become four, five, or six days; the costs are spiraling out of control, and suddenly everything you've planned is out the window. On that day in Pune, when Mr Azad kept us moving, he single-handedly prevented that from happening. Within three hours of arriving at his repair shop, we were on the road again, which is remarkable.

We came across other people like Mr Azad too, people who played key roles in keeping the show on the road, like the guy who interrupted his own journey, and whatever it was he'd set out to do that morning, to lead us back the way he'd just come to find Mr Azad. He didn't speak much English; he just asked 'Mechanic?' and then, having saved the day, he disappeared again before we'd had a chance to thank him or say goodbye. Perhaps he wouldn't have stopped to help us if we'd been Indian or if we hadn't had a distinctive tiger-stripe Mahindra SUV, which most people know is a special tour vehicle.

To me, the fact that someone stopped when he saw that we'd

broken down is interesting in itself, because I've lived in parts of the world where the guy standing at the side of the road, apparently in need of assistance, might be crazy or have a gun, or both. (There's a reason why so many Stephen King-type novels start with someone pulling up on the road beside a stranded traveler and, by page 10, they're in the trunk of their own car.) But throughout all the time we spent in India, we never once felt threatened or uncomfortable, and time and again we came across people who went out of their way to help us. Because of what that guy did for us that day in Pune, I'll certainly stop in future if I see an oil-smeared Indian standing at the side of the road beside a dirty motorcycle.

Things could so easily have turned out differently on that occasion. At best, we could have been waiting at the roadside for an hour or more, wondering what to do. Or we could have driven back into town and wasted time driving around trying to find someone like Mr Azad who could help us. As it turned out, it was our lucky day. Who knows, perhaps the white rat we saw at the temple at Deshnoke really did bestow a blessing on us!

I think a lot of people have a sense that Indians tend toward being lazy. I have to admit that it was an impression we'd begun to develop before that day in Pune. We'd seen a lot of highway patrol officers dozing in the shade by huts beside the road, apparently oblivious, or at least indifferent, to the chaos and carnage all around them; and we'd seen a lot of sleeping gas-station attendants and truck drivers too. Certainly some people's overriding attitude toward work seemed to be: I'll get to it when I get to it. Clearly though, that's not the whole story, or even the major part of it, because as well as the sleeping policemen, there are people like Mr Azad – craftsmen who work hard, are passionate about what they do, and are never going to be wealthy. We'd seen people working efficiently and effectively at the Mahindra factory, and now we'd seen the same thing on an individual, local level too. It was another reason to have hope for India's future.

At 12.30 p.m., the bikes had been fixed and we had to decide whether to abandon our original plan and stay in Pune again that night, or to push on regardless of the late start. In the end, we chose the latter option, did 263 km in just under five hours, and arrived at Kolhapur at 5.30 p.m. – thanks to an unknown motorcyclist, Mr Azad, and, maybe, the beneficence of a white rat.

Chapter 11
From Kerala to Puducherry

Ryan ─────────────────────────────

Kerala is a long, narrow coastal state in the south-west of India that extends for about 39,000 km^2 and has a population of more than 33 million. Statistically, it's considered to be one of India's 'better' states, in that it has the country's highest literacy rate, highest life expectancy (around 74 years), lowest homicide rate, and lowest incidence of corruption.

For thousands of years, Kerala has been a center for the spice trade. In fact, it was spices that brought the Portuguese to India in the late 1600s, and later other Europeans who colonized the country. The land is very fertile – tea, coffee, and cashew nuts are other important crops – and the state produces a substantial proportion of India's rubber, as well as having a thriving fishing industry.

We'd heard that Kerala was beautiful and we were looking forward to traveling along the coastal highway to the southernmost tip of India. We imagined the road would be something like California State Route 1, which runs almost the entire length of California's Pacific coastline, with sandy beaches on one side and mountains on the other. When I thought about it, I could almost feel the wind in my hair – although I realized, of course, that that was never going to become a reality: only someone with a death wish or a profound, unshakeable faith in fate would even contemplate riding a motorcycle in India without wearing a helmet. What I should also have known was that the road that runs the length of Kerala was unlikely to bear much resemblance – if any at all – to what I imagined it would be.

With a population density of 819 people per km^2, Kerala is the second most densely populated state in India. It has around double the population density of India as a whole, three times that of the UK, twenty-four times that of the USA, and an astonishing 204 times that of Canada. There are *a lot* of people in Kerala and, when we were there, a good percentage of them – plus assorted livestock – seemed to be on the congested, single-lane 'coastal road' from which you catch only very occasional glimpses of the sea.

We spent four days on that road doing an average of 20 kph in temperatures of at least 35 °C. There was no cooling breeze coming off the ocean and the further south we went, the hotter and stickier it became. Every morning when I woke up, I lay in bed for a moment with my eyes shut, trying to remember where we were, until a weary, sinking feeling washed over me as I realized what lay ahead for us that day.

As I say, the term 'coastal road' was something of a misnomer. In fact, for most of its length, the road runs beside train tracks and cuts a swathe through dense jungle-like vegetation, which blocks any view you might otherwise have had of the sea. It's true that the coast itself is beautiful, which means that a lot of people visit it and, consequently, that there are a lot of villages and towns along the highway. Inevitably, substantial sections of the road are incredibly congested. Sometimes, we were able to get up to a speed of maybe 60 kph, but we'd have to slow down again after about five minutes, as the proximity of yet another town was heralded by the sound of car horns honking and by increasing numbers of men, women, children, stray dogs, and cows.

After all our upbeat optimism before we hit Kerala, the actual experience of it was soul destroying. We could deal with the heat and even with driving on a road surface that was decimated by huge, crater-like pot holes. But traffic like that kills your momentum, drains your morale, and takes away all the enjoyment of riding a motorcycle.

As we approached each village or small town, we'd slow to 10 kph and, as soon as we'd done so, a bicycle would zip past on the left, or a three-wheeled tuk-tuk would suddenly make a 180-degree turn in front of us. Tuk-tuks can turn on a dime, and they don't have mirrors. So when their drivers spot potential passengers on the other side of the road, they don't look to see what's coming up behind them; they simply dart across in front of all the oncoming traffic, without any apparent fear or understanding of just how close they've come to getting wiped off the face of the earth by a speeding truck or bus.

There were several occasions when, just as I'd pulled out to pass another vehicle, a motorized, three-wheel death trap swung across in front of it to get to the other side of the road. With my heart racing, I'd slam on my brakes, certain that I was going to hit the tuk-tuk. For a moment, my own life as well as the lives of the other drivers, and of anyone else who had the misfortune to be in the immediate vicinity of what seemed to be the inevitability of an accident, really were in the hands of the gods. Every time it happened and we all survived, I came a bit closer to understanding why someone might believe in fate, or perhaps even miracles.

After a few heart-stopping incidents, I gave up trying to pass other traffic, adjusted my speed and sat behind all the buses, trucks, and cars. Colin and I had already learned that when we saw a bus in our rearview mirrors, the best thing to do was slow down, move over so that we were as close as possible to the side of the road, and let it fly past us. None of the bus drivers ever used their brakes. Like massive, barely roadworthy, smoke-spewing harbingers of death and destruction, buses powered through the villages at the same insane speed as they drove on the (relatively) open highway, pushing cars and bikes off the road in front of them, and sending pedestrians scattering in all directions.

Day 01. Our journey started and ended at the India Gate in the center of New Delhi.

Day 01. The Jama Masjid Mosque in Old Delhi, which was completed in 1656, is the largest mosque in India.

Day 04. The dirt road that marks the Rohtang Pass, at 3,979 m (13,054 ft), in northern India. Knowing that the word rohtang means - pile of corpses - doesn't fill you with confidence when you're riding a motorcycle.

Day 06. Our support vehicle, the Mahindra Bolero, travels along dangerous roads as they twist and turn their way up towards the Saach Pass at 4,420 m (14,501 ft).

Day 07. Looking out over the lush and beautiful Chamba Valley in the northern state of Himachal Pradesh.

Day 08. The incredible Golden Temple at Amritsar, in Punjab, north-western India.

Day 08. Indian border guards at the Wagah border crossing with Pakistan near Amritsar.

Day 10. Two men ride on a camel-drawn cart along the highway north of Bikaner, in the western province of Rajasthan.

Day 10. Colin and Ryan struggle to smile while at the Karni Mata Temple, also known as the Rat Temple, in Deshnoke, Rajasthan.

Day 15. A man hitches a ride on the back of a jeep on the road to Vadodara in the western state of Gujarat.

Day 16. The landscape changes to lush green fields and mountains as our team approaches Nashik in Maharashtra.

Day 17. A pillion passenger struggles to keep control of his umbrella during torrential rain near Mumbai.

Day 18. Looking down on northern Mumbai from the 35th floor of a high-rise office tower.

Day 28. Watching the sun set on the beach at Kanyakumari at the southernmost tip of mainland India.

Day 30. The stunning pillars of the Hindu Sri Meenakshi Temple in Madurai, in the state of Tamil Nadu.

Day 30. A man is blessed by a holy elephant at the Sri Meenakshi Temple in Madurai.

Day 40. Fertilizing the crops growing on lush farmland north of Kolkata in the eastern state of West Bengal.

Day 43. Houses cling to the sides of the Lesser Himalaya mountains in Darjeeling, West Bengal.

Day 44. Women pick tea leaves at the Makaibari Tea Estates near Darjeeling

Day 48. A stupa – a mound-like structure containing Buddhist relics – at the Mahabodhi Temple at Bodh Gaya, in the northern state of Bihar.

Day 50. At sunrise, men and women mourn their dead and bathe in the River Ganges at Varanasi in Uttar Pradesh, northern India.

Day 50. Ghats beside the River Ganges in Varanasi.

Day 53. A man takes a photograph of the Taj Mahal in Agra, Uttar Pradesh.

Day 54. After 54 days, we drove along the only really good – and, in parts, empty – road of the entire journey, the Yamuna Expressway, which runs for 165 km (102 miles) between Agra and Delhi.

For a lot of the time, we drove at no more than 15 kph: it simply wasn't safe to go any faster. We were passing through maybe ten small towns and villages every hour – so up to a hundred a day – which meant that our adrenalin was always pumping. That in itself was exhausting, both physically and emotionally, frustrating, and, ultimately, momentum killing. But, however great the stress of driving slowly amongst fast-moving traffic, it was infinitely preferable to coming, repeatedly and literally, within centimeters of killing another human being.

The roads in northern India had been crowded with vehicles being driven too fast by people who lacked the necessary driving skills. But at least on those roads you had the sense that there was some underlying organization; it was almost as if everyone was taking part in a mad but, at some basic level, choreographed dance. In Kerala, however, I felt as though we'd been thrust into a crazy computer game that was completely devoid of rules and logic and that involved us being attacked from every side.

If you manage to survive Kerala's roads, it's actually an interesting province. Primarily Muslim, it has an elected communist state government, and on any particular stretch of road you might see a couple of mosques, a Hindu temple, maybe a Christian church, and a building adorned with a hammer-and-sickle, the emblem of the Communist Party. The people of Kerala are as diverse and interesting as their culture. Some are dark-skinned Indians from the south, and some have light-brown, almost Arabian, complexions – although, in fact, I can only really speak for the men, as most of the women are veiled.

Every night on our journey through Kerala we checked into a hotel on the ocean, and every night it felt like a reward for surviving another hot, dirty, nerve-racking day. Colin, particularly, loves the ocean, so for him it was a huge plus. While we were driving, I'd often visualize the moment when we'd arrive at the next hotel, unpack our bikes, and then throw ourselves into the sea. We'd swim, watch the sun burst into flames before sinking beneath the horizon, talk to the fishermen who were unloading the day's catch from their boats, and be reminded of the many positive aspects of India and of just how beautiful the country is.

It was while we were riding through Kerala that we realized we had to think of India as comprising two completely separate experiences. It's certainly true that, because of the conditions on the roads, it's a horrible place to ride a motorcycle for any length of time. But traveling in the country also involves interacting with people such as the fishermen in Kerala, Mr Azad and the other guys who dropped everything to fix our bikes and enable us to keep moving and stay on the road, and the crowds of grinning, head-waggling, friendly people who gathered around us every time we stopped, and wanted to know what we were doing, where we were going, and why.

During those days in Kerala, there were times when we

hated the trip. When we really thought about it, however, it wasn't India we hated, and it certainly wasn't the inquisitive, almost exclusively supportive people we met along the way. It was just the traffic that sometimes made us wish we were almost anywhere else in the world. Once I'd compartmentalized those things in my mind, I found it all much easier to deal with. It made sense, too, of the fact that most motorcycle touring in India occurs in the mountains, where the population density is relative sparse and where there's much less traffic, or in the centre of the country, where, apparently, the roads are better.

I'm sure that no Indian planning to do a motorcycle journey for pleasure – which many people do – would choose to ride through the country's second most densely populated province, where it makes sense to farm the fertile land rather than cover it with tarmac to expand the existing road network. I just wish I'd done my research a bit better so we'd known the facts before we set out on what, in my ignorance, I'd imagined would be an uplifting part of our journey along a beautiful coastal road. Other people knew what it was really like, of course, and when we were riding through the province and wrote about it on our Facebook page, we had a lot of responses from Indian motorcycle riders saying, 'Oh Kerala! It's really bad – slow moving and dangerous.' Now they tell us!

As well as the lunacy of the drivers, the sheer volume of traffic, the haphazard movements of the pedestrians, the darting dogs, and meandering cattle, there were the pot holes. Before we set out on the Middle Kingdom Ride two years earlier, Colin and I did an off-road course at BMW in Germany, where we learned some skills and techniques that proved to be potentially life-saving. We did the course because the route we planned to take around China was going to involve passing through some very remote regions where the 'roads' would be little more than rough dirt tracks. You expect to encounter pot holes on roads like that. On a national highway in India, on the other hand – or in any other country – you don't anticipate having to maneuver your motorcycle around craters so large they could accommodate an entire SUV.

Paradoxically perhaps, the smaller pot holes where what caused us the worst problems – the ones we bounced in and out of on our motorcycles with our arms constantly pumping and every muscle in our backs stretched to painful breaking point. And all the time, the buses flew past us, so close they almost skimmed our knees, the heat was intense and unrelenting, the tuk-tuks darted in and out of the traffic like demented, suicidal fireflies, and a voice in my head kept asking, 'Why are you here?'

You expect traffic congestion in cities – I'd witnessed it in Delhi when I'd been to India before. What we hadn't anticipated was that it would be equally as bad on the inter-city highways. In fact, it was worse, because whereas you know you're going to have to drive slowly, stopping and starting all the time, in the cities, we hadn't even considered the possibility that we'd have to drive in the same way on major roads away from urban areas.

When you're stuck in traffic doing 10 kph in the sort of temperatures we were experiencing, the air flowing through the ventilation system in your motorcycle jacket is incredibly hot. And when you're body's already cooking and you can barely breathe, your mind isn't as sharp as it would otherwise be, which is a real problem at any speed when kids and dogs and cattle and tuk-tuks are constantly testing fate right in front of you.

At 5 o'clock in the afternoon on day 24, Colin and I pulled over to the side of the road to drink some water and try to breathe. A few minutes later, as Chad and Dan pulled in behind us, I suddenly felt the last remnants of energy drain out of me. We'd been locked for days in a relentless battle against the suffocating heat, the horrific road conditions, and the chaotic, unremitting, incredibly dangerous traffic. There wasn't any part of my body that didn't ache and I couldn't think of one single positive aspect of what we were doing. Foolishly perhaps, I told myself that nothing could possibly happen that would make things any worse. Completely shattered, I lay down on the dusty ground beside the SUV and fell instantly into a deep, exhausted sleep. I don't think anything short of a full-scale hurricane would have kept me awake at that moment.

What I should have known, despite my exhaustion, was that, however bad things are, they can always get worse and a couple of days later, Dan got really sick. As well as being physically worn out, we were all malnourished, and when Dan got food poisoning, his whole body simply shut down. Reaching the point at which he couldn't go on happened very suddenly and I knew we had to find a hotel as quickly as possible. We checked into the first one we came to, which turned out to be horrible; after a sleepless night, it wasn't only Dan who felt even more wretched in the morning.

He kept insisting that he didn't need to see a doctor, but I think it was the prospect of having to stay in that hotel for even another hour that gave him the willpower he needed to drag himself out of bed and into the SUV. Chad drove, with Dan beside him, slumped in the passenger seat with his eyes closed and clearly feeling as terrible as he looked. We'd gone about 100 km by the time we found a decent hotel by the ocean. As soon as we'd checked in, Dan crawled into bed and stayed there for the next two nights, until he was fit to continue the journey.

We were all worn out by that time and we were grateful for a couple of days' rest. Chad, Colin, and I had hit similar barriers before, when we traveled around China, so we already had some idea of our limits and capabilities. But it was Dan's first experience of having his endurance tested on a daily basis. For me, those days when he was sick acted as a reminder that there's a link between physical and mental health, and that, quite apart from any other considerations, challenging our minds and bodies day after relentless day wasn't going to get us safely to the end of our journey.

After a couple of days, when Dan felt well enough to push on, we left the hotel by the sea and drove 100 km to Kanyakumari, at the southern tip of India. It was the halfway point of the India Ride, which seemed an appropriate time to reflect on the previous twenty-nine days. I think I came to two main conclusions. The first was that the moment you start thinking you know something about India is the moment when it's going to reach out and slap you in the face. The second was that the journey had been much more difficult than I'd expected it to be; it was certainly considerably more arduous than traveling around China had been. And that was the real surprise as far as I was concerned, because when we were actually in the thick of the Middle Kingdom Ride, riding a motorcycle around China had seemed to be a fairly tough challenge. Consequently, by the time it came to organizing the India Ride, I thought I knew what I was doing, at least insofar as planning daily distances was concerned. The problem was that whereas in China you can drive 300 km a day without too much stress, in India you're doing well if you manage to cover 200 km. It was a problem that had a knock-on effect and influenced almost everything else, and it meant that when we left a hotel at 9 o'clock in the morning we knew that by the time we reached the next hotel – at around 5 p.m., if we were lucky – we'd be exhausted, but only 200 km further down the road.

As I contemplated the first half of our journey around India, I couldn't decide whether to think of it in the light of, 'The last twenty-nine days have been really hard; the prospect of carrying on for another thirty days or so is daunting, to say the least,' or whether to be more upbeat and optimistic and tell myself, 'That's the difficult bit over; the next half of the journey will be a breeze by comparison.' I tried to convince myself to believe the latter, although I have to admit that I was leaning more towards the first option. I was proud of what we'd already achieved. As I say though, I was also surprised by how unprepared I'd been for the intensity of it all. Perhaps the others were thinking the same thing, although, almost as if by tacit agreement, we didn't really talk about it as a group.

According to popular belief, the ancient and historic town of Kanyakumari (previously known as Cape Comorin), which is at the southernmost tip of mainland India in the state of Tamil Nadu, is the point at which oceans meet, although, in reality, it's surrounded on all sides by the Laccadive Sea. The town's native population of about 20,000 is boosted every year by more than two million tourists, who come to lie on its beaches, walk in the surrounding mountains and forests, and visit its many temples and memorials, including the impressive Gandhi Memorial.

A cooling breeze flows over the peninsula in the evenings and as the fishermen unload the day's catch off their boats, people gather at the port to buy fish and mussels. Then the sky darkens and the red-gold sun grows larger and more brilliant before finally sinking beneath the horizon, to be replaced by a huge silver moon. On the evening we arrived in Kanyakumari, we stood together watching the magnificent sunset and I had a sudden feeling of optimism. It didn't last long though, and as the fading rays of the sun disappeared beyond the water, a malevolent, worry-mongering voice in my head was already muttering, 'Is the worst really over? Or is there something on the road ahead that's going to push you to new limits?'

'Well, whatever lies ahead can't be any harder than what we've already experienced,' I told myself.

When you do a long, arduous journey like the India Ride was turning out to be, you have to 'compartmentalize your objectives', which really just means dividing up the journey in your mind and setting yourself a series of small goals. You have a choice. You can tell yourself, 'I'm circumnavigating India. It's going to take about sixty days. It's now day 10 (or 15, or 20) and I'm already more exhausted than I'd ever imagined it was possible to be.' That might be true, but thinking about it isn't going to get you through all the days that lie ahead. So the alternative is to divide the journey into lots of short, separate stages. Then you can tell yourself, 'It's been hard, but I've completed stage one. Now I just need to get to the end of stage two, and then stage three ...'

Another tactic is to overemphasize all your small achievements. For example, I could tell myself we were at the halfway point of our journey and – the good news – we were on schedule. Of course, if you're battered and shattered, the good news tends to be kicked out of your mind by the potentially less good news and by the questions you're trying not ask yourself, such as, on this occasion, 'How much does keeping to the schedule really matter? Would it be better to add ten days to the precious schedule and go a bit easier on ourselves during the second half? In terms of financial outlay, we're making a TV show and every day is costing several hundred dollars. So is sticking to the schedule simply sensible or is insisting on doing so actually bordering on control-freak obsessive when everyone's completely exhausted?'

In the end, the decision to stick to Plan A was a joint one: after all, surely the worst was over and everything was going to be easier from now on. All we had to do was stop focusing so intently on the schedule; get on our bikes at 8.30 every morning; ride all day and not agonize about how slowly the kilometers were ticking by; figure out any problems as we went along; stop riding at dusk, by which time we should have reached our next hotel; and just get on with it.

As if to prove that my earlier optimism had been well-founded, when we left Kanyakumari the next day and headed north to Madurai, we traveled on a brand new road through the desert and did 254 km in four hours, which was a record for the India Ride.

I'd been to Madurai before, on a photographic assignment,

and I wanted to show Colin the Meenakshi Amman temple. We'd already visited the Rat Temple at Bikaner and the Golden Temple at Amritsar, so maybe the fourteen gateway towers of the Hindu temple that stands on the banks of the river in the heart of the ancient city of Madurai didn't seem quite as remarkable as it might otherwise have done. It is beautiful though, and it's a very spiritual place.

What we wanted to do in all the places we visited was learn about India from the people who live there. It was for that reason we engaged the services of a local – and, as it turned out, loquacious – guide to show us round the Meenakshi Amman temple while Chad filmed it. The problem with 'visiting the sites' on a journey like the one we were doing is that, as a result of the effort involved in moving forward every day, you develop a persistent underlying level of tiredness that dulls your desire to dig deeper and learn anything other than superficial details about the places you visit – even places that, in different circumstances, you'd find really interesting. We were seeing so many things we hadn't seen before and our senses were so overloaded with new sounds, sights, and experiences that I think we'd all reached the point of being unable to focus and fully absorb anything. And, although I know it sounds shallow to say so, I think we'd all have been happy with a brief, non-academic tour of the temple at Madurai.

Before going inside it, we took of our shoes and stood on the hot ground – at least this time there was no rat excrement. What the temple at Madurai *does* have is an elephant, which, although infinitely preferable to thousands of rats, made me a bit wary, I'm ashamed to say. Apparently, being blessed by an elephant is a good thing. So we did what everyone else was doing and held up some coins. The huge creature turned slowly toward us, made that incredibly loud, threatening noise elephants make, reached out with its trunk, grabbed the money out of our hands, and dropped it into a pot. Then it 'blessed us' by laying its trunk on our heads, while I tried to adopt the expression of the sort of man who doesn't flinch at the hot, wet touch of an elephant. Unfortunately, I think there's photographic evidence to prove I wasn't entirely successful.

We left Madurai at 8 o'clock in the morning of Monday, 1st October – day 31 – and arrived in Bangalore, in the state of Karnataka, in the center of southern India, seven hours later, having driven 445 km on a brand new expressway. According to *The Times of India*, the population of Bangalore increased by almost 50% in the ten years to 2011 and currently numbers more than 9.6 million. Going there involved deviating from what would otherwise have been our more direct route up the east coast of the country. We did it because we'd been asked to take part in an event that had been arranged there by Lenovo, one of our sponsors. We had a really amazing afternoon connecting with local bikers from around the Bangalore area, swapping stories about great rides and the best routes for motorcycle touring in India. The next morning, we were back on the road again, heading for the town of Puducherry, about 370 km away on the east coast, where we were going to visit a factory owned by Lenovo and have a chance to learn something about high-tech manufacturing in the region.

The vast majority of the businesses involved in India's IT industry are based in Bangalore, Hyderabad, Delhi, Mumbai, and Chennai, just north of Puducherry. The first IT company to be set up in the country was in Mumbai in 1967. Since then – and particularly during the last fifteen years or so – IT services and business process outsourcing have expanded rapidly and are now important sources of both domestic employment and export revenue, providing direct employment to almost 3 million people and indirect employment to 9 million. Recently, however, the rapid growth in India's IT and computer industries has slowed, due in part to problems resulting from the global financial crisis and, more specifically, to increasing competition from countries such as China and the Philippines. In fact, the Chinese company Lenovo is currently the number one seller of personal computers in India (and the largest PC manufacturer in the world).

I've visited a lot of computer factories in China, and I was interested to see one in India that had been set up by a Chinese company. Once again, what we saw was direct proof of the potential that exists in India and of what people there are capable of doing when their skills are recognized and channeled. It's a country that seems to have an almost infinite number of contrasting facets and we knew that, however long we were there, we wouldn't manage to do more than scrape the surface of just a few of them.

Chapter 12
Death and frustration on the east coast highway

Colin

We were relieved to discover that the expressway from Puducherry to Kolkata is actually quite good. There's still loads of craziness on the road – dogs and cows and mad driving; but at least the quality of the road itself is decent and we were able to travel 486 km up the east coast from Puducherry to Ongole in one day – day 35. The following day, we did 576 km to Visakhapatnam, and the day after that 442 km to Bhubaneswar. It was on day two of that stretch of the journey that we had a brutal reminder of the very real and ever-present dangers inherent in what we were doing.

The road-kill in India is like nothing we'd ever seen. Without any exaggeration, we saw at least ten dead dogs a day – literally hundreds of them during the whole trip. They were mostly dogs that had been hit by cars; often their bodies were split wide open and their exposed guts were being eaten by birds. Having lived in China for so long, Ryan is used to it, to some degree at least; whereas I found it very upsetting. We had dogs when we were children – beautiful Golden Retrievers that were loved and cared for and part of the family – and I've always been a dog lover. As with almost anything though, if you see enough dead dogs on the road, you become desensitized. Even so, it *is* disgusting.

Inevitably, I suppose, people in India aren't sentimental about animals in the way we are in the West. Looking after a dog – feeding it every day and taking it to the vet when it's ill – is a luxury you can't afford when your focus is on feeding your own family. So although I felt sorry for all the dead dogs, I didn't really spare much sympathy for their erstwhile owners. And then, one day, we'd pulled over to the side of the road to drink some water and have a few minutes' rest from the onslaught of the traffic, when we actually saw a dog get hit.

It had wandered onto the road almost right beside us and after the car hit it, it lay there, twitching and kicking one of its legs feebly, until its owner ran out and picked it up in his arms. The poor creature was covered in blood and the man was clearly very distressed about what had happened to it. He carried the dog back to his home beside the road and lay it down gently on the ground. There must have been ten people gathered around it when it took its last breath. Seeing that brought the road-kill back into focus again. It's one thing if the dogs are just stray village dogs no one cares about, but that dog had a name and someone loved it, so you have to assume that at least some of the others did too. It shouldn't make it worse, but somehow it does. I guess culling by vehicle impact is a way of controlling the population of dogs, which would otherwise very quickly reach unmanageable proportions.

Amongst all the other horrible dog-related incidents I saw in India involved a litter of puppies tucked away with their mum at the side of a road in a city. The puppies were simply rotting away – dying of starvation, while a thick swarm of flies hovered around them, waiting. I wanted to stop and save them, but what could I have done? I was just a visitor, on a motorcycle. And if I had been able to scoop them up and feed them, what about all the others? I couldn't fix India; not even Gandhi could do that. And, distressing as it was to see all the dead dogs, it was nothing compared to the trauma of seeing those three dead human beings after the accident on the road to Mumbai. In the West, you can live your entire life without ever seeing a dead body.

There are dangers inherent in driving anywhere, but in most situations in most countries, people consider those dangers to be outweighed by the benefits. I'm not sure that's the case in India, which has the most dangerous roads in the world. What's so frustrating – and I think unacceptable – is the fact that most of the problems on India's roads could be fixed. Doing so would involve reorganizing a lot of the infrastructure, and some of the things that would need to be done would cost a great deal of money; although some of them wouldn't. I know it isn't realistic to think it's possible to solve all the problems on the roads in

India – at least in the short or medium term – but anything would help.

Throughout our entire journey, we rarely saw active traffic police on the roads outside the cities. Why aren't they out there enforcing speed restrictions, stop signs, traffic lights? Why aren't they stopping the trucks that are speeding the wrong way down the expressways and saying, 'You're an idiot; here's a fine'? Why aren't there fences at the sides of the roads to prevent cows wandering onto the highways? Why is it possible to get a driving license without taking a proper driving test, or, in some cases, any test at all?

There was a report in a UK newspaper recently that had the headline 'Police shoot dead runaway cow'. According to the article, 'A cow almost caused mayhem after running on to a busy commuter route ... The road was closed while police caught the animal and made sure drivers were safe.' (It was a small, local newspaper; not the national press!) Obviously, destroying a cow wouldn't be acceptable in India, but the clearly very different attitude in the UK to the fact of an animal being on a road at all serves to highlight the understanding in other countries that it's very dangerous.

One of the huge problems on India's roads is related to truck drivers, most of whom are paid (a fairly small amount of money) per load delivered. Obviously, the faster they deliver each load, the sooner they can pick up another, and the more loads they deliver, the more money they'll earn. It doesn't take a genius to work out that the system encourages them to travel vast distances without taking a break, which some of them are only able to do because they're hyped up on energy drinks, and even sometimes drugs, to keep them awake. So maybe the first step is to introduce fines for truck drivers who break the law and put other people's lives at risk. When you're working long hours trying to earn enough to feed your family, a hefty fine is going to make you think twice about doing something stupidly dangerous.

What I can't get my head round is the faith angle: I don't need to learn to drive because god will decide when I die; we don't need to put up fences to stop animals wandering across the roads and causing fatal accidents, because that's the natural order of things. I guess with a population of 1.2 billion and rising, it might seem to the powers-that-be that individual lives are dispensable. But every one of those lives matters to someone, and it just isn't good enough to shrug, sit back, and let totally avoidable accidents keep happening.

There are multiple different models for this sort of thing. After what we witnessed every day on the roads in India, I just want to sit down with someone in authority there and show them an Excel Spreadsheet of road-death statistics from another country – almost any other country – that does have fences alongside its roads. Surely then they'd see that the solutions to at least some of the problems are just commonsense, and that all it needs to save some of the thousands of lives that are lost in road-traffic accidents every year is logical, intelligent decision-making. India clearly has a lot of problems, many of which may seem insurmountable, but there are numerous quick fixes that would have a huge impact and might even solve some of them. It's like that saying: How do you eat an elephant? Answer: One small mouthful at a time.

I really try not to become bitter on these trips, but, as you can probably tell, I don't always succeed. I did feel bitter at the end of the India Ride, just as I did after our journey around China. Clearly, despite both of them being amazing countries in many ways, they're places I shouldn't live.

All the way up the east coast to Kolkata, the traffic was beyond challenging. The roads themselves were decent, but just imagine driving on a motorway in the UK or on an expressway in North America and having to worry all the time that a cow or a dog might be about to jump out in front of you. Or, even worse, that the rickshaw that's currently hidden by the truck ahead of you is suddenly going to appear around the front of it and do a U-turn directly across your path to pick up a passenger on the other side of the road. You can't ever relax. It's mentally exhausting; and the faster you're traveling, the more exhausting it is. If a car hits a dog, it's likely that no one is going to get hurt, so it only really matters to the dog and its owner. If you're on a motorcycle doing 160 kph, you'll probably slice the dog in two and keep on going.

But when you're doing 80 kph, which was our top speed when we were really motoring, the dog is going to get stuck on your wheels and you're going down.

According to a report in *The Times of India* in March 2013, during the period between 2008 and 2011, road fatalities were reduced in 88 countries worldwide; during the same period, India's roads became more deadly, topping the global charts in 2011 with 143,000 deaths. What other country would just shrug and accept a figure like that? Is it just down to religion, to a belief in god's will? When you're riding long distances on a motorcycle you have a lot of time to think, and I've thought about that a great deal; but I still can't make any sense of it.

There are two lanes in each direction on the National Highway 5, which runs up the east coast of India. At least, that's the idea. What actually happens is that instead of there being two northbound lanes on one side of the road and two southbound lanes on the other – as there would be in any other country in the world that I can think of – people drive in both directions on both sides of the road. Why would that happen? Surely the way it's intended to work is logical, from both a purely practical as well as from a safety perspective. What it means is that when you're driving in the left lane behind a truck and you want to move out to the right so that you can pass it, you have to look ahead of you as well as behind you to make sure nothing's coming towards you on *your side* of the road. What it also means is that a potentially good, relatively safe road is rendered incredibly dangerous – simply because, for some unfathomable reason, people don't do the rational thing, follow the rules, and stay on their own side of the highway. It's that sort of thing that makes me frustrated and angry; I just can't help it.

The vast majority of drivers on the roads in India are men, and most of the truck drivers – who are often the worst offenders of all – are under the age of thirty. It makes you wonder whether something happened fifteen years ago to make someone say, 'Holy cow, we've got a whole bunch of kids with no job prospects. Let's give them licenses and loans to buy trucks. Then they can spend their time traveling around India hauling …' Well, hauling virtually nothing, in fact, because it seems that a lot of the trucks are empty.

Trucks clutter the roads during the day and at night their drivers park up and sleep – sometimes actually on the road itself, with their lights off. But it's all okay, because even if you appear to the uninitiated to be doing everything possible to get yourself killed, you rebalance the odds from time to time by stopping at one of the many little roadside shrines to be blessed by a priest. If time is tight, you don't even need to stop: you can simply slow down and toss some coins in the direction of the bowl that's been placed in the dirt at the side of the road. With your offering made, whether you arrive at your destination or get wiped out in a horrible, avoidable accident along the way is in the hands of the gods.

That sense that people are absolving themselves of all responsibility made us so angry it became difficult to turn off our bitterness at the end of the day. We had to keep reminding ourselves that it wasn't India we hated; it was the behavior of the truck and bus drivers, particularly. India is an amazing place and there were a lot of things we loved about it. But driving there is like playing some super-fast, full-on computer game: you're being attacked from every direction, your brain's working overtime, and the stress of it all is making your heart race. The only difference is that if you fail to avoid an attack in a computer game, you just start again. In the real world in India, however, there's a very strong possibility that you won't get that chance.

In Kerala, although the traffic was bad, the road went up and down mountains; so, with the exception of the superfast buses that plough their own furrow down the center of every highway, was relatively slow moving. On the east coast, where the land was flat, the trucks were doing 80 or 90 kph without ever slowing down. I guess when you've got poor brakes and a tuk-tuk turns directly in front of you or a kid steps out onto the road, there's no point even trying to stop.

On day 38, after traveling 2000 km in four days, we went to the Chandaka Elephant Reserve at Bhubaneswar, in the state of Orissa. Ryan had wanted to visit a tiger park, but when we applied for permission to film there, we were turned down, apparently because they were renovating. So, determined to have some animal-related element in our journey, he looked for something else. It had to be something that was on our route because we were getting towards the end of the India Ride, we were tired, the roads were dangerous, and traveling any unnecessary additional distance would have increased the already substantial risks. Then he found the elephant park.

We'd already paid a fee to film there and although we hadn't really known what to expect, the place seemed a bit bleak. We'd expected the elephants to be roaming free within the confines of the reserve and that we'd be taken by car to watch from a distance while they were feeding. What actually happened was that we sat in a clearing amongst the trees and waited for 35 or 40 minutes until they brought us four massive elephants with chains on their legs. It was all a bit strange. But we fed the elephants and petted them – at least, Daniel, Chad, and I did. Despite it having been Ryan's idea to include a nature element in our journey, he has a fear of wild, semi-domesticated, and even some domesticated animals.

It was the extremely loud noise the elephants made that particularly unnerved him on this occasion. That, and the fact that no one provided a satisfactory answer to his, not unreasonable, question: 'What's stopping them crushing me to death with their tusks?' Having temporarily overcome his very strong resistance to standing anywhere that was within several feet of the elephants, Ryan fed one of them a coconut – which made it trumpet even more loudly than it had been doing. A few minutes later, the same elephant reached out its trunk and ripped a massive branch off a tree. I guess that gave Ryan the answer to his question: 'Nothing.'

The next day (day 39), we did 453 km to Kolkata on a good expressway, and the day after that we visited an amazing hospital in the south of the city – the Vivekananda Mission Ashram Netra Niramay Niketan Hospital (VMANNN), which since the early 1990s has offered community-oriented hospital services to an underserved region of rural India. The hospital specializes in eye care and provides approximately 14,000 surgeries annually, based on a model whereby local people pay – or don't pay - according to their means.

In the early 1990s, there were estimated to be 35 million blind people in the world; more than a third of them lived in India, where, due to a number of factors, cataract blindness is particularly prevalent – and almost entirely curable. From 1995 to 2002, the Cataract Blindness Control Project, supported by the World Bank, not only prevented millions of people in India becoming blind, but also instigated the building of many new operating theaters and eye wards and the training of ophthalmic surgeons. Those surgeons are now some of the best in the world, partly as a result of the fact that they perform a high volume of cataract operations compared to their counterparts in the West.

Today, as well as being a training center for doctors from

India, Europe, and North America, the VMANNN hospital just outside Kolkata incorporates a boarding school for sighted children and a school for blind children, funded largely by the charitable Seva Foundation, which is based in San Francisco, USA. When we arrived, the children from the blind school were all lined up to welcome us. We were asked to 'launch' a bus that was going to be sent out around the community to educate people about eye care and when we cut the ribbon, all the kids cheered. It was a really touching moment.

As it turned out, I think that hospital visit did more for us than we did for them. It was late in the journey and we were the sort of tired that's just a few short steps away from wretchedly miserable. So it was uplifting to be part of something that was full of goodwill, incredibly well organized, and positive. It certainly went a long way toward restoring our energy and optimism. In fact, it was one of the most special things any of us had done – not just during the India Ride, but ever. What we saw that day was another of India's faces; it was one that the people of India should be immensely proud of.

We'd heard that the roads north of Kolkata were better, whereas the truth is that they're worse – maybe because there's less commerce in the north so there's less need for good roads. It was starting to get really hot too. That first day out of Kolkata – the day after our visit to the hospital – we'd hoped to reach Maldah, about 400 km away, but that proved to be a bit overambitious. The first road *was* pretty good for about 50 km; then the expressway ended and suddenly we were riding through flooding, over rocks, and in and out of massive potholes. All the time, we were battling against the erratic craziness of the truck drivers and the honking buses that seemed to be intent on forcing us off the road or into the path of other vehicles. By the time the sun began to go down on day 41, we'd realized we weren't going to make it to Maldah and we decided to stop for the night at Pakur.

For most of that section of the trip, we were driving along the border with Bangladesh, and certainly some of the kids who wandered beside and occasionally onto the road must have been refugees. None of us had ever seen poverty on the scale we saw there. There's poverty in every country, of course; but in China, for example, people who are poor generally have at least something to eat and a roof of some description over their heads. In West Bengal, the deprivation was clearly on a completely different level. In 2006, Pakur was listed as one of the 250 most backward districts in India – out of a total of 640. It's ironical, perhaps, that since 1977, when a coalition Marxist-Communist government was first elected in West Bengal, living standards have apparently declined there and the gulf between rich and poor has widened.

It wasn't just the people and the traffic that slowed us down this time though: it was the road construction too. In most countries – certainly all the ones I have any experience of – when a new road is being built, a route is created around it. It might just be a dirty, dusty track with a single lane controlled by traffic lights, but it keeps things moving. In India, there doesn't seem to be a protocol for that sort of situation; they simply leave people to work things out for themselves, which means no lights, no alternative route, and, before long, no moving traffic. And when the truck drivers, who are apparently totally lacking in foresight at the best of times, don't have anywhere to go, the gridlock that develops can take literally hours to clear.

Perhaps it's because Indians have a different concept of time that they tend to be so patient. I don't mind waiting for a legitimate reason – if there's an accident, for example – but having to wait for a stupid reason makes me mad. All it needs when there's road construction is for someone to put up a traffic light so that cars going in one direction have right of way for five minutes, and then cars going in the other direction have priority. They don't do that in India, so it ends up in a potentially lethal game of chicken before it all grinds to a halt and no one goes anywhere. I guess even if someone did put up a traffic light, the drivers wouldn't take any notice of it unless the police were there to enforce it, which is unlikely, as no one ever seems to enforce anything in India.

I sound bitter and negative, I know; I don't want to be, particularly when there were so many incredibly positive and heart-warming aspects of India and we met so many amazing people there. It was just that being stuck in a completely unnecessary traffic jam was infuriating and epitomized another, totally unfathomable, face of a country of many contrasts and contradictions. But I suppose people everywhere do stupid things that seem inexplicable to the people who do different stupid things, because we all do *something* stupid, whether it's smoking, drinking too much, or jumping off a mountain attached to a parachute and to some guy you've just met and about whom you know absolutely nothing!

It was on day 36, as we rode up to the hotel entrance in Visakhapatnam after doing 576 km in extreme heat, that a couple of security guards almost physically tackled us. It was dark and these guys came running after us shouting, 'Stop! Stop!' When we did stop, at the hotel entrance, one of them grabbed me by the shoulder and almost yanked me off my motorcycle. I was startled and annoyed, and I flicked out my elbow instinctively. And that was when Ryan completely lost it. Pulling off his helmet and throwing it down on the ground, he started screaming. For about sixty seconds there was mild but total chaos. I knew just how Ryan felt: you lose your perspective after a day like that. Then the hotel manager came running out, apologizing profusely, and told the security guards to back off.

They're all just foolish incidents really, in the greater scheme of things, and they pale into insignificance in comparison to the really dangerous ones: being frustrated to the point of losing your cool is one thing; nearly killing someone is something else entirely, as I was soon to discover.

'Pushing on' was at the back of our minds for most of the time every day. Whenever we hit particularly bad traffic or a poor-quality road, we'd start wondering, 'Are we going to reach our destination before it gets dark?' It was a constant concern that became more urgent as soon as the sun began its descent towards the horizon. On day 41, it was almost dusk when we decided to pull out our phones and look on the internet for the nearest hotel with a website.

We found a place in a town called Pakur that looked okay and we were heading for it, driving through a tiny village just as the last of the day's light was leaving the sky, when a kid jumped out in front of my bike. We must have passed hundreds of kids that day, playing at the sides of the roads and running around just inside the limits of our peripheral vision. I was always aware of them and I always drove defensively, with all my senses alert, waiting for one of them to do the unexpected. I didn't see this little girl though, until she was there on the road, right in front of me.

I braked and swerved but I was certain I was going to hit her. My heart was thudding against my ribs and I felt physically sick. As I swerved, I almost dropped the bike, but then I was passed her, and she was just a reflection in my mirror. By some miracle, at the very last moment, when an impact seemed inevitable, her mother had managed to yank her back off the road. Fortunately, we'd been going slowly – as we always did when passing through the villages. If I'd been traveling just a couple of kph faster, I'm certain I'd have hit her.

I was shaken and upset by what had happened. I don't think I'd have been able to live with the guilt if I'd seriously injured or killed that little girl. What I'd also realized, though, was that, if I'd stopped, I'd probably have very quickly been surrounded by people. I'd seen the child's mother smack her across the face after she'd dragged her to safety. But I suspected that her sense that her daughter was to blame for what had almost happened would have given way to fury with me if things had turned out differently. There were hundreds of people on the road and in the shacks beside it, and the situation could quickly have become overwhelming. So I was glad that we'd kept going.

As it got darker, my feeling of unease continued to grow. At last, we reached Pakur, where the hotel was. Even when there were directions on hotel websites, they were never good, and we had to stop and ask someone the way. We turned the corner the man had indicated and began to drive slowly down a very dark alleyway when a thought suddenly struck me: 'What if this is a trap and there are people waiting in the shadows to rob and kill us?' Clearly, the near-miss incident with the child earlier in the day had really thrown me; although, in fact, it wasn't a completely implausible possibility when you consider that we were a couple of expensively kitted-out foreigners riding motorcycles in a very impoverished area. In the land of the blind, the one-eyed man is king.

As it turned out, there were no robbers lurking in the shadows, and the hotel was relatively new and nice enough. I'd have settled for much less that night. I was just glad to unload the bikes and get off the streets, which, thanks to my state of increasing disquiet, had begun to feel extremely unsafe. I reached a very low point that night. I was totally exhausted – mentally as well as physically. My whole body was shaking, I looked like the walking dead, and I couldn't make myself relax. During the course of 'normal life', you don't have to psyche yourself up into battle mode on a daily basis. In fact, you rarely, if ever, even have reason to elicit your fight-or-flight response. After a ten-hour day on the motorcycle, constantly having to fight the traffic and avoid hitting all the people and animals on the road, I think that almost hitting that little girl and then fearing for my own life had tipped me over into a state of shock.

There were a few times during the India Ride when I'd had enough: that day was one of them. As had been the case in China, there tended to be fewer of those moments as the journey progressed; I guess I reach the point when I think, 'I've come this far; I might as well keep going for the last few days.' In the early days of the India Ride, there were several occasions when I asked myself, 'What are you doing? How did you get yourself into this again?' And there were times when I did actually regret it. The truth is that I regretted a lot of the trip while I was doing it. It was only when it was all over and I was out of it that I thought, 'That was great.' But I imagine that's normal whenever you do anything really difficult.

Chapter 13
Darjeeling

Ryan ─────────────────────────────────

I'd heard good things about Darjeeling. I was looking forward to visiting a tea plantation there, and to breathing the cool, clean air of the mountains. In the 1800s, when India was a colony of the British Empire, a sanatorium and military base were set up in the Lesser Himalayan Mountains, in what was later to become the Indian state of West Bengal. When plantations were subsequently established in the region, Darjeeling became known for a distinctive type of black tea.

Our visit couldn't have come at a better time: we'd had a tough few days and we all needed a rest. So when we woke up in Siliguri on the morning of day 43 of the India Ride, I couldn't wait to drive out of the relentless heat and humidity of the plains into the cool, crisp mountain air. I think we all felt the same way, and the mood was light as we ate our breakfast, packed up the car and the bikes, and then hit the road. It wasn't going to be a long drive – just 80 km from Siliguri to Darjeeling – so even though we made quite a late start, we expected to arrive by early afternoon at the latest. That would give us time to check into our hotel, clean ourselves up, and have a leisurely stroll around the town before dinner. But, of course, we didn't cruise up the mountain and arrive in Darjeeling in time for lunch. I don't know why I believed, even for a moment, that everything – or, indeed, anything – would go according to plan. I'd like to think it was a belief born of innate optimism rather than an inability to learn from past experience.

The fact that trucks and buses aren't allowed on the narrow mountain road to Darjeeling had misled me into believing that it would be fairly clear of the sort of traffic we were getting used to. I hadn't anticipated the apparently never-ending stream of SUVs that wind their convoluted way through the mist. What actually happened was that we spent six hours weaving a slow, tortuous, and acutely frustrating path up a vertical, twisting, switchback road in intense heat and an unbelievable volume of traffic.

Another misconception we'd all had was that Darjeeling itself would be a peaceful town and relatively empty of people. We'd been on the road in India for more than forty days: we should have known by then that even the mountainous regions are densely populated.

So, just to recap: we set out from Siliguri in the morning full of optimistic anticipation, looking forward to a not particularly easy but at least relatively traffic-free ascent into the mountains, where we would spend three relaxing days in a really nice hotel, recovering from all the days that had gone before, and recharging our batteries so that we were ready to face the challenges that lay ahead.

And the reality? We had a long, exhausting journey on a road that was congested with traffic and so steep and twisting that, long before we reached our destination, the muscles in my arms were burning from the huge effort required to keep the motorcycle upright as I maneuvered it around what seemed to be an infinite number of perilous bends. Then, just as the road began to straighten out and driving became easier, I had a flat tire.

The problem I'd had in Rajasthan had been due to a slow leak and, by pumping up the tire, I'd managed to limp into the nearest town. This time, however, it was a full-on puncture and I quickly realized I wasn't going anywhere. Until that moment, the fact that houses line almost the entire length of the road that runs, pretty much vertically, up the mountain to Darjeeling had seemed like a negative, because of all the people, cows, dogs, and bicycles that have to be constantly monitored for any sign that might indicate they're about to do something dangerously irrational. Now though, the existence of all those houses became a good thing, because where there are houses and small shops, there is also likely to be someone who can quickly fix a flat tire on a Royal Enfield motorcycle.

It didn't take us long to find a couple of truck-tire repairmen who were working in a small, open-fronted, tin-roofed shack.

I'd assumed a puncture in a truck tire would be pretty much the same as a puncture in a motorcycle tire. But I was wrong. Fortunately, there was a motorcycle-tire repair shack not far away, and inside it was the silver lining to the dark cloud that had been frustrating our attempts to reach Darjeeling, because if I hadn't had the puncture, we wouldn't have had the very positive experience of meeting Kelsang.

A Tibetan-looking Buddhist with an Elvis Presley haircut, Kelsang is passionate about motorcycles, speaks great English, and likes to show off his pet chicken. When we explained what had happened and told him about our journey, he immediately laid aside all his other work, found and fixed the puncture in superfast time, showed us his stamp collection, talked to the camera like a pro, and single-handedly restored our previously exhausted good humor.

Thank you, Kelsang. You're a good man.

It was dusk by the time we reached Darjeeling and the fact that we were all physically and mentally shattered made it even more disappointing to discover that it bore virtually no resemblance to the Himalayan nirvana I'd imagined it to be. To say it was crowded with people would be a massive understatement. To put it in some sort of understandable context: in an urban area of about 12.7 km^2, Darjeeling is home to approximately 132,000 people, which is more than 10,000 people per km^2. If that still doesn't enable you to imagine just how crowded it is, perhaps some comparisons will clarify things.

The population density in Toronto (which is currently the cause of some concern amongst Canadians), is around 4000 per km^2; in Greater London, it's about 4500 per km^2; and in New York City there are 4600 people per km^2. That means that all those 'really crowded' places actually have fewer than half the number of people per square kilometer than are living in the small Himalayan town of Darjeeling.

As I say, Darjeeling is crowded! But at least the hotel was good, the air was cool, and for the next three days we'd be getting the downtime our minds and bodies so desperately needed.

Apart from its tea, Darjeeling is also well-known for its narrow-gauge railway – the Darjeeling Himalayan Railway, or Toy Train – which runs for just under 80 km to New Jalpaiguri railway station in Siliguri. The track, which was completed in 1881, is right next to the road and rises from 100 m above sea level to about 2200 m. Most of the trains are now pulled by modern diesel locomotives, but some vintage British steam engines still remain as a tourist attraction. I imagine it's a cool way to get up the mountain – it certainly has to be easier than riding up it on a motorcycle.

That evening, we ate a good meal at our hotel and slept well in comfortable beds, and the next morning we visited the Makaibari Tea Estate. We knew almost nothing about tea before we went to Darjeeling, and although we were mildly interested in it – in the way you are about learning anything new – I don't think any of us were expecting the visit to be riveting. In fact, tea growing and processing are a great deal more interesting than one might think, and we had an awesome day.

Until about ten years ago, there were tea plantations all over the Himalayan foothills around Darjeeling. Then auction prices fell and many of the estates were forced to close. But the people at Makaibari – which has been owned and run by the same family since it opened in 1895 – were determined to find some way of carrying on. By introducing sustainable organic agricultural methods and fair-trade principles that benefit both the environment and the local community, the estate has recently been revitalized. The tea that's grown there is still picked and sorted by hand before being dried and processed, again without the use of modern machinery.

In terms of mechanization and production processes, almost everything about the Makaibari Tea Estate is as different from the car factory we visited in Pune as anything possibly could be – and, in its way, it's equally successful. What's also different about the tea plantation is that a substantial proportion of its workforce is women, who do all the plucking and sorting of the tea. In most of the other areas of India we'd passed through, women had been notable by their absence, certainly in any commercial or working environment. So we were impressed to see so many local women employed at Makaibari – although slightly less so when we were told, 'Women do the jobs that require patience and are therefore not suitable for men'!

The workers on the tea plantation are paid a daily wage, regardless of how much tea they pick, sort, or process, and everyone who works there lives on the estate, which extends over hundreds of square kilometers of spectacular mountainside. I've photographed tea plantations in China, so I knew it was going to be a visual experience, but I had no idea just how beautiful it would be.

We were shown around by the general manager, Kuldip Basu, who told us about the processes involved and the different types of tea they produce there, including Silver Tips Imperial, which is the most expensive tea in the world. We tasted white tea, silver green, second flush muscatel, oolong ... Although I don't have a sensitive-enough palate to be able to differentiate between the various qualities, they certainly all tasted different – and very good. For a few hours, the road seemed to have been relegated to another world.

The next day – day 45 of the India Ride – was a full rest day. No one worked; we all just slept, ate, and relaxed in the cool, clean, mountain air. Not being on the road also gave us a chance to talk to people and I chatted to some Indian motorcyclists who were staying in the hotel and who had some interesting insights into life and politics in India.

'Indians are very educated people,' one of them told me,

'but for some reason they don't choose good leaders. That's the tragedy of our country. We have the "raw materials" in terms of the people themselves, and then a lot of that potential is wasted in the hands of weak and corrupt politicians. And globalization hasn't helped us.'

I don't know enough to have any real opinion about Indian politicians, but I'd certainly been impressed by the skills as well as the language abilities of many of the people we'd interacted with since our journey began. I could see the guy's point about globalization too, particularly when Colin tried to buy an Indian tea set in Darjeeling to take home for his wife and found that, stamped firmly on the base of every cup and saucer he examined in every shop were the words 'Made in China'.

While Colin and Daniel were shopping, Chad ran in the hotel gym, and I sent off some of the film we'd taken to our production team in New Zealand. Then we all met up for pizza.

The town itself was noisy and crowded with cars and people – a microcosm, in fact, of all the things I struggled with in India. But everything there has at least one other side to it and, in this case, the contrast was epitomized by our hotel. An old colonial mansion in a previous incarnation, the hotel was an oasis of comfort and calm that I almost didn't want to venture out from. After spending three nights there, all worries about dying on the roads had become a distant memory and we felt rejuvenated. It was good to put on a sweater and jacket again, for the first time in almost thirty days, and not to look as though I'd spent several days trapped in a filthy, oil-stained chimney, as I'd done when we arrived.

When we left Darjeeling on the morning of day 46, we'd pretty much be on the home stretch, on a route that would take us through the state of Bihar and then west to Delhi. We'd reached the point in our journey when it had become even more important than ever not to drop our guard: we had to stay alert if we were going to get back to Delhi safely and in one piece. The last few days of any long trip are often the hardest and most stressful, not least because you can't help thinking about home and seeing your family again, so your mind is no longer completely focused on the journey itself. It was the thought of all of us staying safe that was occupying *my* mind as we left Darjeeling, dropped down from the mountains, and headed back into the heartland of northern-central India, which is one of the most densely populated parts of the country.

Chapter 14
Ancient India

Colin

Whenever we told anyone we were planning to travel through Bihar, they all said the same thing: 'Don't! It isn't safe. It's a really poor province – the Wild West of India.' Almost invariably, they'd illustrate the point with a story about someone they knew who'd been robbed at gunpoint or car-jacked there. 'If you *have* to go to Bihar,' they'd say, 'avoid gas stations where there are men just standing around. A lot of people get robbed at gas stations.'

Obviously, we were a bit concerned. Then we read in a guidebook: 'The extreme poverty and general lawlessness of Bihar can make buses and private hire cars targets for bandits, who periodically use mock accidents and road works to stop vehicles.' And that made us a bit more concerned.

Apparently, the activities of Maoist and other militant groups add to the dangers in Bihar, and although tourists aren't thought to be specific targets (which was at least some small comfort), the advice was to avoid traveling after dusk. I guess every country has at least one particularly crime-ridden city – based on crime statistics, it's Detroit in the USA and Glasgow in the UK. But most of them don't have a whole state.

I'm not really afraid of being hurt physically, which might just be because I've never been beaten up, and maybe you don't really fear something like that until it's happened to you. What I *was* fearful of was having our film footage stolen. Ryan had sent a lot of it from Darjeeling to the production team in New Zealand, but we'd done more filming since then, and whereas bruises and even broken bones will heal, losing the additional footage and all our expensive camera equipment would be a much bigger problem.

We had a choice: we could either ignore all the dire warnings people had given us and travel straight through Bihar, or we could backtrack on what we already knew to be a horrible road, skirt the southern border of the province and then drive north again – which is the route we would have taken if we hadn't wanted to go to Darjeeling. We were very close to the end of our journey and we didn't want to have to deal with any additional obstacles; we just wanted to get home safely and be done with it. So, in the end, we decided against any kind of detour: we'd go through Bihar and just be super-cautious.

According to a recent study from Oxford University in the UK, 55% of the population of India lives in poverty; that's around 645 million people and about one-third of all the world's poor. Contrary to what most people probably believe, there's more acute poverty in India than in many African countries. In fact, in eight Indian states – including the northeastern states of Bihar, Uttar Pradesh, and West Bengal – the poverty is greater than it is in the twenty-six poorest countries in Africa. In Bihar itself, 81% of the population can be considered to be poor based on a Multidimensional Poverty Index that includes child mortality, nutrition, drinking water, education, and sanitation. Those are shocking statistics. Clearly, to people living in those sorts of conditions of abject deprivation, we were extremely well off by comparison, with our motorcycles, SUV, and costly equipment – and that was another discomforting thought.

At a lot of the little towns in India, you're charged a sort of city tax in the form of a toll, which you pay to guys who stop you on the road. There's usually a barrier, although it's kept raised because of the constant flow of traffic. Other than that, there isn't any real signage, and the 'tax collectors' don't wear uniforms. Perhaps they're really just local gangs running an ad-hoc scam. Motorcyclists don't normally have to pay, but our support vehicle did. In view of all the stories we'd heard about Bihar, however, we decided we'd all just power through every time without stopping. After all, we were four good-sized men who were aware of the dangers. What could go wrong? For once, fate apparently wasn't tempted by the question: people were incredibly nice to us and everything was fine. Maybe we were just lucky.

There was one moment when we thought some guy was following us. We hadn't forgotten any of the stories we'd been told, and I started thinking, 'He's been behind us for a long time. He must be planning to rob us.' If it had been anywhere else in India – Kolkata, for example – I wouldn't have thought anything of it at all. Of course, he turned out to be just some guy going about his business, which happened to take him in the same direction we were heading.

We'd driven from Darjeeling in West Bengal to Bhagalpur in Bihar on day 46. The next day we were still in Bihar as we traveled south-west to Bodh Gaya, where we had an off-bike day before continuing in a north-westerly direction to Varanasi, an ancient town on the River Ganges in the province of Uttar Pradesh. Although, throughout the four days we were in Bihar, we didn't ever feel physically threatened, we did feel claustrophobic and on edge because of the huge volume of people and traffic, the unremitting sound of blaring horns, and the incredible heat. It seemed that Bihar was more crowded, noisier, and hotter than all the crowded, noisy, hot places we'd visited before.

Obviously, a lot of the poverty in India is a result of overcrowding: there are simply too many people, which was something that was particularly apparent in West Bengal and Bihar provinces. While we were traveling, Ryan and I discussed the theoretical pros and cons of some sort of state-run family planning, and compared the situation in India with that in China, which has a one-child per family policy. Although, instinctively, it seems wrong for the state to tell people how many children they can have, the situation that exists somewhere like Bihar makes you wonder if there are circumstances in which it might be a good idea. The problem is, of course, that the argument becomes more complicated if you factor into the equation things like freedom and fairness.

Perhaps, in the longer term, the answer lies in education. Apparently, there are charitable initiatives in Bihar to educate girls; we certainly saw a lot of girls in school uniforms while we were there, which is something we didn't see elsewhere. Education, literacy, and the potential to have a career before starting a family might be a slower route toward reducing the birth rate and thereby alleviating some of the poverty, but empowering people and enabling them to make their own informed choices certainly seems to be a better way of achieving the desired outcome.

Of course, in India, every coin has at least two sides, and girls in Patna (the capital of Bihar province) were recently banned from using mobile phones – because they were 'debasing the social atmosphere'! How do you make any sense of that? All you can say, once again, is that India is a country of contradictions and a place where some bizarre, seemingly random stuff happens.

We saw another of Bihar's contrasting faces at the Mahabodhi Temple at Bodh Gaya. Some time between the 6th and 4th centuries

BC, a sage called Gautama Buddha, who was also known as Siddhartha Gautama (Siddhartha means 'he who achieves his aim'), sat under a tree in Bodh Gaya and vowed to remain there until he'd found the truth and obtained enlightenment.

There's certainly a lot of profiteering in religion, but there are also vast numbers of people who gain strength from their faith, some of whom have extremely hard lives and need something to believe in. So, despite being non-religious ourselves, Ryan and I have respect for other people's religious beliefs, however crazy they might seem. And of all the religions I know anything about, Buddhism is the one I actually find interesting, particularly in terms of its underlying principle of doing no harm, although even Buddhism goes off at a bit of a tangent and makes what's basically a story into something rather more complicated. Because of that interest, however, I was looking forward to visiting Bodh Gaya, which, for Buddhists (of whom there are estimated to be between 350 million and 1.6 billion worldwide), is the holiest place on earth.

We rolled into Bodh Gaya at dusk on Wednesday, 17th October (day 47 of the India Ride) and the next morning we went to the Mahabodhi Temple. Standing on the banks of the Falgu River, the temple was built beside a 'descendant' of the tree, now known as the Bodhi tree, under which Buddha was sitting when he received enlightenment. There's some disagreement about the date of construction of the temple, but the original structure is believed to have been founded by the Indian Emperor Ashoka, about 200 years later, and then excavated and restored in the late 1800s by the British archaeologist Sir Alexander Cunningham.

We were shown around the temple and the seven spots where Buddha meditated by an excellent guide called Nadeem, who possessed a sharp sense of humor. We'd already obtained permission to film there, and the temple manager and his staff were welcoming and enthusiastic about what we were doing. The temple was clean, well run, and beautiful, and the whole experience was a very good one. In fact, Ryan and I agreed that the Mahabodhi Temple was even more interesting and unique than the stunning and very moving Golden Temple at Amritsar.

After lunch, we drove about a kilometer to a Vipassana Meditation Center to do some meditation training. Having spent forty-nine days on the road, we were, inevitably, quite stressed out, and it seemed like a good time to go in search of some inner peace.

When Ryan first made contact with the guys who run the center, before we set out on the India Ride, they'd asked him, 'Are you interested in the three-week program or the full six weeks?' When he told them, 'We just want to come for a couple of hours,' they'd obviously thought he was making a joke and had laughed, politely. They were less amused when they realized he was serious, and they were frankly dismissive when he told them he wanted to bring a camera crew. Although he did manage to persuade them in the end, they were clearly still skeptical about why we wanted to film there.

The man who manages the meditation center and who met us when we arrived there has a really interesting story. He used to work in the World Trade Center in New York City, as an executive for a large Indian-owned multinational company, and he should have been on one of the planes that crashed into his office on 9/11. It was a flight he caught regularly, but something had come up elsewhere that morning that needed his attention. So, not only was he not on the flight, but he was also away from his office, thereby, in effect, cheating death twice. He quit his job the following day and it was while he was trying to figure out why he'd lived that he went to the meditation center at Bodh Gaya – and ended up helping to run it.

He showed us round a beautiful, very peaceful compound, which contains two dormitories (men and women are segregated to avoid distraction), a main meditation hall, and a Buddhist temple. Vipassana is a particular type of meditation – the word means to see things as they really are – which is taught at 148 centers and more than 100 other non-centers around the world. Many of the people who do the courses have experienced traumatic or otherwise life-changing events; others simply want to take a break and give themselves the time and mental space to think about what they're doing with their lives, and whether they really want to be doing it.

All visitors to the center have to leave their possessions at the door – and, symbolically, their emotional baggage too. They aren't allowed to bring in phones or computers or to communicate with the outside world in any way. Apparently, when they first arrive, many people struggle to meditate for even an hour, but by the end of their stay they're able to do anything from eight to fifteen hours a day. For people like Ryan and me, who have to keep moving, that's a challenging prospect, particularly for Ryan, who needs constant stimulation, never sits and chills, and only ever watches a movie when he's strapped into the seat of an airplane 30,000 feet above the ground.

Despite his initial reluctance, the manager of the center agreed to give us a 'taster' meditation session. After our tour, he took us into an empty meditation hall, where we sat on the floor and he told us, 'Close your eyes. Try to clear your minds and concentrate on your breathing.' After visiting the Mahabodhi Temple that morning, we'd gone back to the hotel for lunch, and we were about to learn our first lesson: don't try to meditate on a full stomach, because you'll simply fall asleep.

When Ryan needs to think, he goes hiking in the mountains in China, and any interest he might have in meditation would probably be for the same reason some people do SAS training: to test himself by doing something that's completely outside his comfort zone. He said later that he managed to clear his mind for about thirty seconds before dozens of thoughts, ideas, and strange memories from the past rushed in to fill the void like a swarm of agitated, noisy bees. He tried to swat them away and concentrate on his breathing, but they just kept coming. Then he found himself wondering if other people have a similar experience the first time they attempt to meditate, or whether it was just him and he was insane.

I fared a bit better than my brother, perhaps because I'm more used to making time to think: I usually do it during long walks, listening to jazz through headphones, and I've also had a few sessions in isolation tanks. However, walking while thinking is quite a different thing from trying to focus on your breathing and not think about anything, which, in reality, is even more challenging than it sounds.

We only managed about thirty minutes, after which I expected Ryan to say, 'That was the most inefficient thirty minutes of my entire life. Do you have any idea how many emails I could have written in that time?' In fact, what he actually said was that if he was ever forced to stay in a meditation center, it would be like being put in jail, and that after just ten minutes, his back had started ache, his legs were cramping, he was uncomfortably hot, and he felt that he'd failed on every front.

The experience was made only slightly less disheartening by the manager of the center telling us that people always struggle for the first few days, and then they get over the hump and go on to gain something positive from the experience. And, despite the challenges of sitting still and trying to control our thoughts, visiting the center did have a peaceful, calming effect and gave both Ryan and me a new respect for the process of meditation. I left there thinking that when I got back to London, I'd find my nearest meditation center and give it another try. I haven't managed to do so yet, but maybe one day.

When we left Bodh Gaya, we traveled north into Uttar Pradesh, to the ancient city of Varanasi on the banks of the River Ganges. According to legend, Varanasi was founded by the god Shiva. It's certainly one of the oldest inhabited cities in the world and, to Hindus, the most sacred of all sacred sites.

Hindus believe that bathing in the River Ganges – which is at the very heart of Hinduism – will wash away their sins, dying in the city will bring salvation, and scattering the ashes of cremated bodies on the water will release the soul. After traveling around India for forty-eight days, Ryan and I had learned to expect the unexpected. Despite our determinedly open minds and the almost palpable spirituality of Varanasi, however, we were surprised and appalled by how dirty it was.

When we arrived in the city, on the evening of day 49 of the India Ride, Daniel was sick again. In fact, we were all feeling really rough, but we got up early the next morning and by 6 a.m. had joined the throng of people who'd already congregated at the ghats, the stone-slab steps that lead down to the water. There were people swimming, bathing, and brushing their teeth in what must be some of the most polluted river water in the world in a temperature that, even at that time in the morning, was about 38 °C.

As the sun rose over the river, Ryan and I did what a lot of the other tourists were doing and hired a boat. The ancient part of the city is comprised of a phenomenally beautiful labyrinth of narrow lanes, which are lined by shops and Hindu temples and teeming with people and the ubiquitous cows. Sitting in the little wooden boat on the water, we looked back at the mismatched buildings and could almost feel the history. It was as though all the people who'd gone there over the centuries to cremate their dead and scatter the ashes in the holy River Ganges had left behind them some sort of ethereal presence.

There are approximately 100 ghats in the city. Many are privately owned, most are used for bathing, and some are for cremation. In the past, the custom of throwing dead bodies into the river caused terrible cholera epidemics, and now only the ashes of cremated bodies and bones are allowed to be scattered on the water. But the cost of the wood required to burn a body completely is way beyond the means of many people, and, inevitably perhaps, it's another rule that isn't always adhered to. Consequently, a pragmatic solution has had to be found, in the form of a species of turtles that feed on dead human flesh and that are bred and released into the water to consume the partially burned remains.

Although Ryan and I did discuss bathing in the Ganges, we imagined that, by day 50, our immune systems would be so weak that even one previously un-encountered bacterium might have an effect that would land us in hospital. I know that, for Ryan particularly, if potentially disease-inducing pollution alone hadn't made swimming in the river out of the question, the turtles would certainly have done so.

As we'd discovered during our circumnavigation of China, the last part of a long journey is probably the toughest part in many ways, including trying to focus on what you're experiencing when all you really want to do is stay on the road and get home. In Bodh Gaya, we'd been quite buoyed up by what we'd seen; just a couple of days later, we'd reached a plateau of exhaustion that made it difficult to be truly interested in anything. Suddenly, getting some rest became our most urgent need, and we returned to the hotel at lunchtime, had something to eat, and then slept for five hours. When we woke up, we had dinner, and slept again for another ten.

Despite our extreme tiredness, however, we left Varanasi the next morning with a sense that we'd seen somewhere special, even though, unfortunately, it wasn't an uplifting experience. Maybe the very close association between the city, the river, and death was what dragged our spirits down. We were glad we'd gone there, but none of us was in the right frame of mind or had the mental energy required to interact with people in the way we'd have liked to have done.

We knew before we set out on the India Ride that we wouldn't learn a great deal about the country. Riding a motorcycle for eight hours every day to the point of near-collapse isn't conducive to gaining any really meaningful knowledge; all it allows you to do is get an impression of a place and of the people who live there. What we hadn't expected after fifty days on the road, however, was to have more questions than answers. We began to realize that the more we saw of India, the less we knew about it.

Chapter 15
The return to modern India

Ryan ───────────────────────────────

When we set out again on the morning of day 51, we were just a couple of days away from Delhi and the end of our journey. At that point, you get goose bumps when you think about how close you are to completing your epic journey. You have to keep reminding yourself to pull back and that most fatal accidents happen within just a few kilometers of people's homes. 'Stay focused,' we kept telling each other. 'Don't let your guard down or something bad will happen. Don't forget, we haven't finished yet.'

We did 347 effortless kilometers that day, spent the night in a hotel in Kanpur, and did another 292 km to Agra on day 52. The most memorable event of those two days was probably my getting stung by a bee. It hit my neck while I was riding my motorcycle and fell inside my shirt. I must have crushed it when I thumped my chest with my fist, but it was too late: it had already stung me. Fortunately, I managed to keep control of the bike as I slowed down and pulled over to the side of the road. Only then did I allow myself to release the 'Ouuuuch' that had been building up inside me. Then I ripped open my jacket and swatted the dead bee out with my hand. It had got me right on the collarbone and a huge red welt was already spreading down onto my chest. You can't really complain too much when your only injury after fifty-one days on the roads of India is a bee sting, but it really hurt.

When we arrived in Agra, it already felt as though we'd re-entered modern India. We checked into a good hotel that was full of well-heeled tourists – both Indian and foreign – most of whom were staying there for just a day or two while they visited the Taj Mahal. With our thick, unruly beards and once silver-grey/now almost-black, oil-stained motorcycle suits, we must have looked as out of place as we felt.

Agra was the first really big international tourist site we'd visited throughout the entire journey. At the Wagah Border with Pakistan, most of the other visitors had been Indian; at the Golden Temple at Amritsar they were primarily Sikh pilgrims; and at the temple at Bodh Gaya they were almost exclusively Buddhists. Now, suddenly, in Agra we were thrown back into the realms of global tourism. It was a reminder – had we needed one – that we were just 200 km from cosmopolitan Delhi.

At the hotel, we cleaned ourselves up and then sat on the rooftop terrace drinking wine and watching the sun set over the Taj Mahal. It was an emotional moment, for many reasons, and in some ways it might have been the more natural end to our journey. Somehow though, it seemed more fitting to close the circle and finish it where it had begun, in Delhi.

The next morning we went to the Taj Mahal. It didn't matter that there were what seemed to be a million tourists there: it was stunning. The many photographs I'd seen hadn't done it justice and, in fact, it was far more impressive than I'd expected it to be. It should definitely be on everyone's list of 'places to visit before I die'. Although we were too tired to explore as much as we might otherwise have done or to take in everything we read on the signs, I enjoyed immensely the time we spent there.

Built in the mid-seventeenth century on principles based on Persian and Mughal architecture, the central focus of the Taj Mahal is the pinkish-white marble dome above the tomb of Mumtaz Mahal, the third wife of the emperor Shah Jahan. As well as marble from Rajasthan, the building incorporates jade and crystal from China, and precious stones from Tibet, Afghanistan, Sri Lanka, and Arabia. It really is spectacular.

We woke up the next morning knowing that we were just hours away from the end of our journey; getting on the bikes was an emotional moment. We were looking forward to doing the last leg of the India Ride on the brand new Yamuna Expressway, which had only been open for a couple of months. A controlled-access, six-lane road, built by an Indian company named Jaypee, the Yamuna Expressway extends for 165 km from Agra to Greater Noida, which is about 50 km from New Delhi and where the first Indian Formula 1 Grand Prix was held in 2011. The problem was that when we set out from our hotel in the center of Agra that morning, we couldn't find the entrance to this modern miracle.

They'd told us at the hotel, 'You'll see the sign; you can't miss it.' And although the road was clearly visible on the map, we couldn't find the entrance to it. We ended up heading off in the wrong direction – toward Delhi, which seemed logical at the time. After we'd been riding for about twenty minutes, were well out of Agra, and still hadn't seen any sign to it, Colin and I stopped to talk about what we should do. There were other roads that would take us to Delhi, but we wanted to end our journey on one that, from what we'd heard, epitomized all the potentially positive aspects of India's future in terms of what can be done there when people put their minds to it.

We looked again at the map and this time we realized that the entrance to the expressway wasn't on the Delhi side of Agra at all, but on the opposite side of town. Not prepared to give up, we decided to backtrack. It was a pain in the ass, but it was worth it. It cost us the equivalent of about $3 to travel just over 150 km on the flattest, smoothest, best road in India. After everything we'd been through during the last fifty-two days, I'd happily have paid $100 for the privilege.

Paying to travel on good roads is a concept that I think should be universally accepted. To build and maintain high-quality roads costs money. So put up toll booths, collect money – it doesn't have to be a lot – from people who are prepared

The return to modern India

to pay to use a good road, and then use that money to make improvements to the country's infrastructure. It makes sense; I've been saying so for years!

Driving on the Yamuna Expressway for two and a half hours on the last day of the India Ride was beyond exciting. There are walls at the side of the road to stop people and animals wandering onto it, and a central barrier to divide vehicles driving in opposite directions. The road was virtually empty, except for a small number of trucks, SUVs, cars, and the occasional tourist bus transporting people between Delhi and the Taj Mahal. In fact, on long stretches of it there was no other traffic at all, and Colin and I were able to weave back and forth across all three lanes, reveling in the space and safe in the knowledge that, for the first time since the wheels of our motorcycles had made contact with Indian tarmac, we weren't in any imminent and very real danger of being hit by a truck or a bus. Suddenly – on the final day of the India Ride – riding our motorcycles became a true pleasure.

When we left the expressway, we followed the road into Delhi and to the Gate of India – from where we'd set out, full of excited anticipation and confidence born of naivety, fifty-four days and more than 12,000 km earlier. I think we all had a huge sense of achievement, as well as a feeling of relief that we'd made it back to Delhi alive and well. We were exhausted, but exhilarated. It would be two more days before we'd fly home to be reunited with our wives and families – me to Shanghai and

Colin to London. We couldn't wait.

For nearly eight weeks, we'd been tested on a daily basis by physical illness, mental exhaustion, crazy traffic, and intense heat – on many occasions, almost to breaking point. Making our way round India on motorcycles had been a grand idea, and I think there was a part of me that was amazed – and perhaps surprised – that we'd actually made it. It was a good feeling, knowing that we'd set ourselves a difficult task and we'd completed it, safely and, in the end, efficiently. By the time we were standing once again at the India Gate, we felt pretty confident that we could do almost anything we set our minds to doing.

When photographs had been taken and we'd got some film footage of the journey's end, we had a nerve-racking thirty-minute drive to the hotel, where Colin and I did our last video diaries, showered, ordered pizza, and went to bed at 8.30, shattered but jubilant.

While you're on the road, you're kept alive by the massive amount of adrenalin that's pumping round your body. Your eyes are constantly scanning your environment for potential dangers; your mind's processing every visual image and sound; and every single muscle in your body is tense and ready for action. The moment you allow yourself to relax, both your body and your mind fall apart: your limbs turn to Jell-O and you can't concentrate or focus your thoughts. It's like making a small hole in a fully inflated balloon and watching the air seep out of it.

The next morning, we returned to the barbershop we'd visited before we set out on the India Ride. All four of us had grown impressive – although untidy – beards during the trip, and the guys at the barbershop remembered us and laughed when they saw us again. I was the only one who opted for full removal of all facial hair – I'd promised my wife I wouldn't go home with the beard that had been allowed to grow, unchecked and unruly, for the last fifty-four days; Colin, Chad, and Daniel just had a trim. We left the barbershop once again fit to take our places in the civilized world, which is when we knew that the journey was really over.

All that remained to be done before catching our flights home was to hand over our motorcycles to the winners of the competition that had been organized by Mountain Dew, one of the companies that had sponsored the India Ride. It was as a development of the social media aspect of our journey that the idea came about to hold a competition with Mountain Dew and give away, as prizes, our Royal Enfield motorcycles. To enter the competition, people had to post photographs on a website of something adventurous they'd done. Colin and I chose the winning images and met the two winners while we were in Delhi at the end of the trip. Then, after we left, the bikes were repaired and tuned up, and ownership was transferred to the two people we hoped would go on to use them with the same kind of adventurous spirit that had led Colin and me to undertake the India Ride.

Chapter 16
Lessons and legacies

Ryan

We thought circumnavigating India would be easier. It's smaller than China, we'd be traveling about two-thirds of the distance we'd traveled on the Middle Kingdom Ride in approximately the same number of days, and a lot of people in India speak English. They were just some of the reasons for believing that, having cut our motorcycle-adventure teeth in China, India would be challenging but not as difficult as it was. In reality, it was *so* much harder, more soul-destroying, uplifting, frustrating, dangerous, and satisfying than we ever could have imagined it would be.

Perhaps one of the most important of the many lessons we learned in India is that every country has its own particular set of challenges. You just don't know what they are until you get there. Of course, not knowing what you're going to have to deal with doesn't mean you don't have to assess what you perceive to be the potential problems and then plan for them. You take with you on every new trip everything you learned on the last one, but each time there'll be new lessons to learn, and every day will be different from the day before. Even on a journey lasting fifty-four days, no two days were the same, and on day 54 we faced problems we hadn't previously encountered. Every trip has new highs, new lows, and new levels of intensity. The only constant is you, and even you change as a result of each new experience.

What's really important is that every day you focus on *that* day. On a long journey like the India Ride, you have to compartmentalize it – break it down into smaller goals so that you're not overwhelmed by the enormity of what you're trying to do. Colin and I found the video diaries helped us to do that. However exhausting and emotionally shattering a particular day had been, we took it in turns to sit in a hotel room at the end of it and talk to the video camera about what had happened. Then we switched the camera off, locking the events of that day inside it, so that when we woke up the next morning, those events were in the past and we could concentrate on pumping ourselves up and starting again.

The film-making aspect of the journey slowed us down and was sometimes exhausting, especially in the last few days. But filming was a large part of the whole point of being there at all, so there was no useful purpose to be served by being petulant and saying, 'This is my trip, man. I just want to get on with it.' If Colin and I didn't round that corner again to allow Chad to film the amazing vista that was spread out in front of us, we wouldn't get the chance to show it to other people, and then all the hard work and money that had gone into the filming side of things would have been wasted. I think dealing with that was sometimes easier for me than it was for Colin.

At no time did I allow myself to forget we were making a show and that getting that footage was important, no matter how painstaking the process. If I had to choose between riding for ten hours to get some amazing footage and riding for eight hours without it, I'd choose the former every time. Part of the reason for that is because I know that, six months after the trip has ended, I'm going to sit down and watch the TV show and think, 'We really did something.' To get that pay-off, I have to play the role of producer, which can be hard to do when you're the one who has to make a plan for filming and stick to it, however exhausted you are. Planning, researching, executing – it's what I do and I really enjoy it.

There were days when I'd be half-asleep in the back of the car and I'd hear Daniel say to Chad, 'Wow, this trip is really well organized.' Knowing they were aware of my efforts and appreciated them gave me a huge sense of satisfaction.

I also really liked the idea of exploring with my brother a country that was new to both of us. Every day for fifty-four days, we shared the difficulties and talked about what we were going to do and how we were going to do it. That collaboration was something that hadn't really happened to the same extent in China, because I'd already been to most of the places we visited.

It felt good to know we were able to work well together and get things done.

Chad and Daniel shared hotel rooms and would sometimes stay up late to watch the day's footage, but Colin and I always went to bed early – driving a car is a lot different from riding a motorcycle. My brother and I shared hotel rooms for fifty-four nights and didn't argue once. Even though there were inevitably moments when we pissed each other off, we always managed to swallow our pride and cooperate with each other. I'm proud of that, particularly as the India Ride might turn out to be the last epic journey I make with my brother. These trips aren't any part of Colin's career – he likes the business of doing business – and when it comes to planning the next one, he might not be able to take time out from his 'real life' and go with me; or he might not want to assume the risks any more. So I'm glad we've shared the experiences we've already had.

I'm lucky, too, to have a very understanding wife. Jasmine knows that I don't ride a motorcycle because I don't want to be with my family. It's true that I like spending time with Colin: he's probably my best friend as well as my brother, and with him living in London and me in Shanghai, I don't get to spend a lot of time with him in the normal course of events. Ultimately though, what I want to do is produce something. So, for me, the journeys are work, as well as adventures. Jasmine appreciates that and can identify with it. I think reading our book *The Middle*

Lessons and legacies

Kingdom Ride was the game-changer for her.

By the time we started planning the India Ride, we hadn't yet produced the documentary or the book about our circumnavigation of China. So we didn't know whether we were going to recoup the very significant amount of money we'd spent, or if anyone other than our friends and families was going to be interested in what we'd done. It wasn't until we found a corporate sponsor and money started coming in to fund the new trip that it became easier to persuade people that we weren't just wasting our time.

I enjoy having the opportunity to interact with the people we meet while we're traveling; I enjoy pushing myself to discover my limits; and I enjoy the creative process involved in planning the trip, executing it, and then sharing it with other people. I guess the last aspect is one of the reasons why I became a photographer: when you take a photograph, there's a moment when you see the image in your mind; then you capture it and sell it to a newspaper or a magazine so that other people can see it too.

Those are all general aspects of doing a journey like the India Ride. But there were also other issues with regard to India specifically. One of the main lessons I learned from India was that you think you know something one day and the next day it turns out that you don't really know anything at all. The more you find out, the more questions there are. I didn't know much about Hinduism, Sikhism, Islam, or Buddhism – the four main religions in India – and I don't know much more now. And I certainly don't understand India's democratic system. I live in China, a country where the Communist government quashes any form of political competition. So, for me, the fact that the Communist Party was able to win a democratic vote in West Bengal and Kerala is incomprehensible. I studied political science and political theory at University of Toronto; I guess I didn't learn much about how and why things work the way they do in India.

What I also don't know is why some things in India don't work better than they do. Why does the power go off every night from 7.30 till 8? Why are so many people killed on the roads year after year and still no one seems to do anything to enforce the existing laws or introduce new ones that would save at least some of those lives? There's so much goodwill in India, so much human power, and so many people who are passionate about their country. Why aren't those resources tapped into in order to make life better for people? Is it lack of money and/or political will? Or is it simply deeply held religious beliefs that result in the abdication of all personal responsibility and an almost total dependence on the fickle finger of fate?

We met some amazing people on the India Ride and we saw some truly extraordinary things. Overflowing with color and life, ridiculously overcrowded, chaotic, frustrating, and constantly surprising, India is a strange, enigmatic place full of contrasts and contradictions. It was never going to be possible for us to understand it in just fifty-four days; I don't think I'd be able to do so in fifty-four years.

One of the reasons Colin and I did the India Ride was in the hope of inspiring other people to have adventures. For me, that's certainly a motivating aspect of any journey. Obviously, doing a protracted motorcycle trip around India isn't going to be feasible for everyone. But a weekend spent driving into the countryside and seeing something new, in fact anything that pushes you to do something different or outside your own particular comfort zone, constitutes an adventure too.

It's easy to develop tunnel vision so that you focus only on what's most immediately important and relevant to your life – your family, your job, your house, your car. Sometimes, you need to take a step back and give yourself the time and space to think about the path your life is taking, and whether it's the path you thought you'd chosen at the outset, or one you've drifted onto without even noticing.

Social media – which is perhaps one of the most influential aspects of the modern world – played a very important role in the India Ride. When Colin and I traveled around China, we didn't have the opportunity to share our experiences in real time. Although the Chinese are online, most people in China don't speak English, and they don't have access to Google, Facebook, or Twitter; instead, they have the Chinese internet site Sina Weibo. So, although we had a website and a Facebook page for the MK Ride, they didn't get used very much, which meant that we weren't able to connect with many ordinary Chinese people. For the India Ride, however, things were very different. A lot of Indians speak English and they are definitely online, with access to all the global websites that are used to share stories worldwide.

One of the first things we did when we were setting up our journey around India was create a website, on which we put brief biographies, a map of our route, and details of all the different equipment we'd be using. Then we made a Facebook page, which we updated every day with news, photographs, and links. The goal was to let our families, friends, and anyone else who might be interested know where we were at any given time, and also to show any Indians who might have forgotten, how amazing India is, which we hoped would encourage them to think about exploring their own country. In the event, it worked really well; so well, in fact, that we ended up with 100,000 followers, the majority of whom were Indian.

There was very little response to our daily posts to begin with, but after day 6 or 7, when we started having some difficult days in the mountains, the interest built steadily – I guess everyone likes a bit of drama. By day 20, we had almost 50,000 followers and started getting anything from twenty to a hundred comments every day. Whenever we mentioned our next destination, people posted advice about that particular region, or just said, 'I was there a couple of years ago. You guys are lucky.' Other people wanted to know about the motorcycles – how much they cost us, or how well they were performing. It was exciting and encouraging to know they were caught up in what we were doing. Those updates were the last thing we did every night and it was fun to wake up in the mornings and check out the comments people had added.

I know some people think that sharing information about something adventurous you're doing is grandstanding – a symptom of being self-absorbed. But it's the sharing of an experience in any way possible that, for me, turns it from something fun into something really exciting. If what I've done inspires someone else to do something they've always dreamed of doing, that *has* to be a good thing, surely. I guess I'm not the only person who thinks like that, otherwise Facebook wouldn't currently have more than *one billion* active users worldwide!

On a more personal level, what the internet also allowed us to do was connect with our families every day – except for one night, when we were in the mountains and had no internet or phone reception. We were grateful for that, and for knowing that they didn't have to worry about us as much as they did last time, when we were traveling around China and were sometimes unable to talk or send messages to them for days on end. They might have been a bit more worried and fearful for our safety, however, if we'd told them the truth about what the roads in India were really like!

Colin ────────────────────────────────

Visiting the Taj Mahal signified the end of the trip for me. It felt like we'd accomplished something and were heading home. We'd seen so much by that time that our senses were overloaded, and I'd expected it to be a bit of an anticlimax. But, as with almost everything in India, it wasn't what I'd expected: despite having seen it in a hundred photographs, it was a very powerful, special experience.

When we left Agra, we rode on the new, almost empty expressway to Delhi, which proved to be the easiest ride of the entire trip. In some ways, that was a positive experience too; in other ways, it was very frustrating. The fact that the road had fences at the sides to prevent the random, potentially lethal wandering of cattle, adults, and children means that some people, at least, know what's required – and they know how to build a good, safe road. So why don't they replicate that elsewhere? Obviously it would cost money, but you're talking about the possibility of saving thousands of lives every year. Why don't people insist on that, rather than apparently simply accepting the huge annual loss of life that results from avoidable accidents on the road?

I guess part of the answer is related to a loose interpretation of Maslow's hierarchy of needs: the first priority is to spend money on feeding people; once you can feed people, you put roofs over their heads; then you educate them ... Clearly, road construction comes pretty close to the bottom of the list.

Another part of the answer is to do with bribes and kickbacks, which, apparently, are embedded in the business culture of India. While we were in Kolkata, we had dinner with one of my former classmates from HULT International Business School in London, whose family builds roads and who told me, 'Out of every $100 of the budget for building a road, maybe only $10 is spent on actual construction.' I don't know what the real figures are; he was simply illustrating the point he was making. It makes you wonder what India could be like if they used, say, $80 for road building and just $20 for kickbacks.

As I think I've said before: lots of questions; very few answers.

Will anyone ever take the long-term view, which is what's so desperately needed if anything's going to change? Maybe not; maybe things will stay as they are and continue to oscillate precariously around the point of disaster. Unfortunately, one thing I can see happening is a massive exodus of rich Indians to the West, to live in cities that are less crowded and have better basic infrastructure. Although India's currently a good place to make money, there are better places to spend it, which is a shame, because it means that wealthy people with good skills won't stay there long enough to make a difference. There's a wide gap between the rich and the poor in every country; in India, the gulf between a multi-millionaire and someone living in a shanty town in Mumbai is so huge as to be unimaginable to most of us.

Despite its gross domestic product (GDP) growth topping 10% a year in 2010, India's currency fell to record lows in August 2013, as investors rushed to withdraw their money and reinvest it in the strengthening US economy. In fact, during the last three years, India's growth rate has halved, to approximately 5%. Unfortunately, while the country's economy was booming, in an attempt to boost its popularity prior to the next election, the government used the money that had been invested in India to provide a wide range of subsidies and to fund what has become the world's most extensive welfare state. It was money that could have been used to create jobs for the millions of young men and women entering the workforce so that they didn't need state welfare or subsidies, and so that India could overtake China as the world's leading source of manufactured goods.

Looked at from a purely practical viewpoint, I don't see that there's any real hope for the country. So maybe one of the main lessons I learned from the India Ride is: be wary of investment in India, and make sure you work with partners you can really trust.

Before I traveled with my brother around China in 2010, I just wanted to make money – as much of it as possible. That was really my only goal. Then I made quite a bit of it, but it didn't feel amazing, as I'd assumed it would do. Of course, it's easy to sit back with cash in the bank and say, 'It isn't all about money'. That's true if you have the luxury of being able to afford to pay all your bills and put a roof over your head. But making money and spending it can't be life goals in themselves.

What it comes down to is the fact that we all have the same basic objective in life: to be able to provide for ourselves and our families. It's very humbling to talk to a farmer in India or China and realize that that's his only aspiration: all he wants to be able to do is put food on the table and educate his children so that they can have an easier life than he's had. If he can achieve that, he'll be content. We talk about 'being happy', but maybe that's what it's really all about – simple, honest, straightforward, and sometimes difficult-to-achieve contentment.

I have a friend who does extraordinary things, and when he was rowing across the Indian Ocean recently, he told me that fourteen days into a fifty-seven-day expedition, the only thing he cared about was food. He was sleeping for two hours, rowing for two hours, and having to take in up to 10,000 calories a day, and he said that life had been stripped back to its barest essential – which, for him, was food, just as it is for the farmer trying to scrape life from the dry, barren soil in an Indian village.

During the hours we spent every day in India on our motorcycles, there was plenty of time to think and reflect. Seeing the miserable circumstances in which some people live certainly reminded me how lucky I am and helped put my life in some of sort perspective that maybe I wasn't really aware of before. You get a lot of self-awareness when you spend two months with your head in a motorcycle helmet. What I also learned from all that introspection was that I was very lucky to have been born in Canada to the parents I was born to, and that I'm no different from anyone else. So I guess the message is: be happy; enjoy your life, and do something with it.

Six weeks of getting up day after relentless day, battling the intense heat and trying to stay alive on the roads, arriving at a hotel, doing a video diary, having a shower, eating something, and going to bed knowing we had to wake up the next morning and do it all over again, became completely exhausting. It's a tiredness that's way beyond any other level of tiredness you might experience in the normal course of life, and it's compounded by all the highs and lows.

Some days I'd feel a huge, almost euphoric sense of achievement because of what I'd accomplished. One very positive aspect of doing a journey like the India Ride is that it teaches you some good life skills and, because everything else seems easier by comparison, it makes you willing and able to tackle almost any challenge with confidence. On other days, I'd feel lower than I'd ever imagined it was possible to feel: not only had I had to face all the physical and mental punishment that particular day had loaded onto me, I was also carrying all the emotional baggage from the previous days. You try to deal with the lows quickly so that your mood doesn't affect the rest of the team; but sometimes you can't.

We had a rule on the India Ride: whatever happened during the day and however weary we felt at the end of it, the first thing we did after we'd checked into a hotel was record our video diaries. Sometimes, we'd feel so shattered and dejected it seemed like a huge imposition, but it did actually help, because it enabled us to unload our frustrations rather than holding onto them overnight and allowing them to fester and grow.

For me, traveling around India was 100% more arduous and exhausting than traveling around China had been, largely because of the sheer number of people and the volume of traffic. Although the traffic was sometimes crazy in China too, they have laws there, and people who are employed to enforce them; so it wasn't the constant struggle it proved to be in India. Of course, the fact that people in China rarely do anything that's against the law because they're terrified of the police isn't a good thing. But maybe the wives and husbands, mothers and fathers, sisters and brothers, sons and daughters of the tens of thousands of people who die on the roads in India every year might sometimes wonder if there's any way to make Indians care about breaking traffic laws. Maybe India suffers from something that's a global problem too: the more people there are, the less difference each individual feels he or she is able to make; so, ultimately, why bother trying?

Liberty and democracy are great concepts, but look at what China's been able to accomplish during the last fifty years without them. The fact that they've done some terrible things is indisputable and indefensible; at the same time, however, they've raised 400 million people out of poverty. Because they don't have democratic elections every four years – and they don't have to start campaigning for the next election after just two years in office, as is the case in the USA – Chinese politicians can plan fifteen years in advance with limited distraction. What that means is that they can actually get things done. In China, the people in power don't have to win any votes, so they don't have to court popularity; whereas in the West, no one who wants to run for office for a second term is going to try to force people to understand the unpopular notion that they have to sacrifice today in order to ensure a better tomorrow. In fact, people can't be forced to accept that: look what happened when they tried it in Turkey and Brazil – there were riots!

I guess my final thought, now that I've had time to reflect on and digest the digestible aspects of the India Ride, is that if I were to do another motorcycle trip, it would have to be a short one. I don't like the filming aspect; I don't enjoy being on camera, not least because, for me, it detracts from the adventure. In fact, I find it more tiring than actually riding the motorcycle, particularly when I have to give an update and I'm not in the mood for talking. The truth is that if it had just been me and Ryan traveling around India on motorcycles, we'd have completed our journey in half the time. So although I still love traveling and adventures, I don't know whether I'd do another journey that involved filming, or being away from my wife and my life and work in London for so long.

It's different for Ryan: having adventures and photographing or filming them so that he can share them with other people is what he does.

It was good to spend the time with my brother, and there are two things about which we are in total agreement. One is: never set out to travel any significant distance on a motorcycle without a rain suit. And the other: India is an amazing, multi-faceted country of contrasts and contradictions with a population of friendly, potentially highly skilled people whose future may depend, to some extent at least, on whether or not they have the will and the ability to take their fate – both individual and collective – into their own hands.

Acknowledgments

We owe a great deal to all the people who made the India Ride possible and to those who have helped and supported us in other ways.

The INDIA RIDE team
Chad Ingraham, Daniel Milton, Deepak Chaturvedi, Jane Smith, TL Lim, Meeyian Yong, Kyle Murdoch, John Crawford, Jack Woon, Alex Stoloff and Jon Hogan.

The wonderful people who helped along the way
Consulate General of India – Hong Kong, Kapil Arora, Deepanker Mukerji, Caroline Rowe, Jasiv Salusa, Puneet Gaur, Himalayan Extreme Center, Daglas, Anil Kapoor, Parnjeet Singh, Harpreet Singh, Gia Duncha, Punit Sheth, Shruti Sengupta, Meenal Kansara, Mr Azad, Goutam Mondal, Dr Shoumya Jyoti Datta Mazumder, Kelsang Wangar Bomyan, Kuldip Basu, Nadim Akhtar, Baskaran, Kashi Ram.

Our corporate partners
Mandarin House Language School: Jasmine Bian.
REV'IT!: Egbert Egbers, Rineke Berkelder.
HULT International Business School: Stephen Hodges.
Zenith Watches: Juliette North, Maud Tiberti, Ping Ong, Ivy Tsai, Cyril Bedat.
TAG Heuer Eyewear: Sophie Pottecher, Diana Hor.
Government of Canada: Simon Cridland, Smriti Saxena, Ritika Nandkeolyar.
Cardo Systems: Michael Goren.
HALO: Anthony Abell, Steve Tocker, Sean Welch, Julian Preston-Powers, Jeff Meers.
Mahindra: Bijoy Kumar, Vinod Nookala, Rajesh Dubey, Venecia Paulose.
The Westin Gurgaon: Sanjay Sharma, Vineet Mahajan, Sukhdeep Bahra.
The Westin Mumbai: Lance Ourednik, Mohit Kanwal, Pooja Vaswaney.
Lenovo: Aditya Agarwal, Parneet Kaur, Tamanna Tasneem, Shrikanth Dhanakshirur, Rahul Agarwal.
Mountain Dew: Ruchira Jaitly, Deepika Warrier, Tarun Bhagat, Suvid Bajaj, Navneet Monga.
SEVA Foundation: Jack Blanks, Aaron Simon.

The India Ride

2 brothers - 2 bikes -
14,000km
around India

---

www.TheIndiaRide.com
facebook.com/TheIndiaRide

MKride

2 brothers - 2 bikes -
18,000km
around China

---

www.mkride.com

facebook.com/mkride

Mandarin House 美和汉语

www.MandarinHouse.com

Learn Chinese today!

The first global Chinese language and cultural educational center

---

Adult courses, corporate programs HSK exams, internship and summer junior courses

With schools located in

Shanghai - Beijing

www.MandarinHouse.com
facebook.com/mandarinhouseschools